# COLOR WITH ME

## Illustrated by Chiquanda Tillie

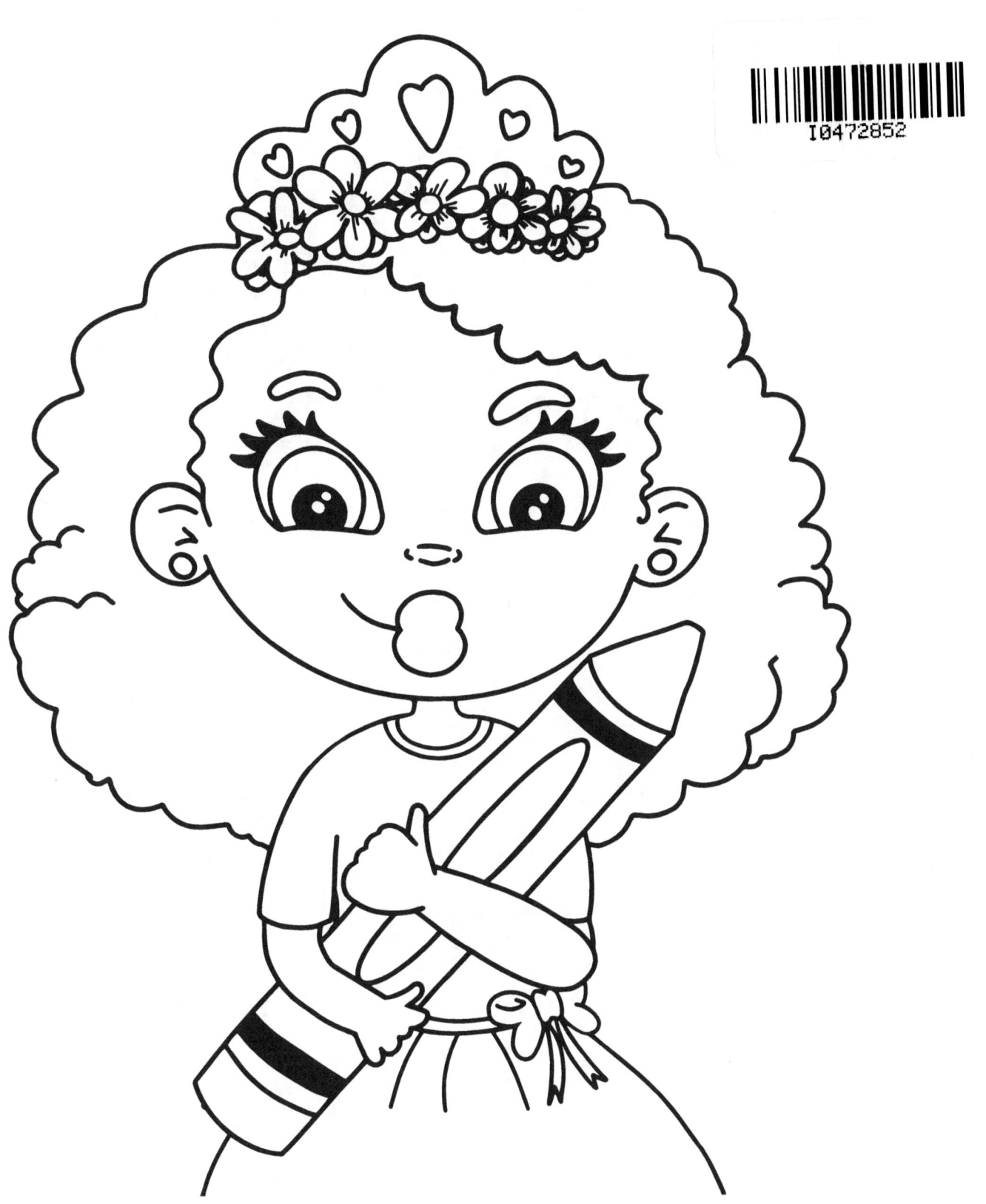

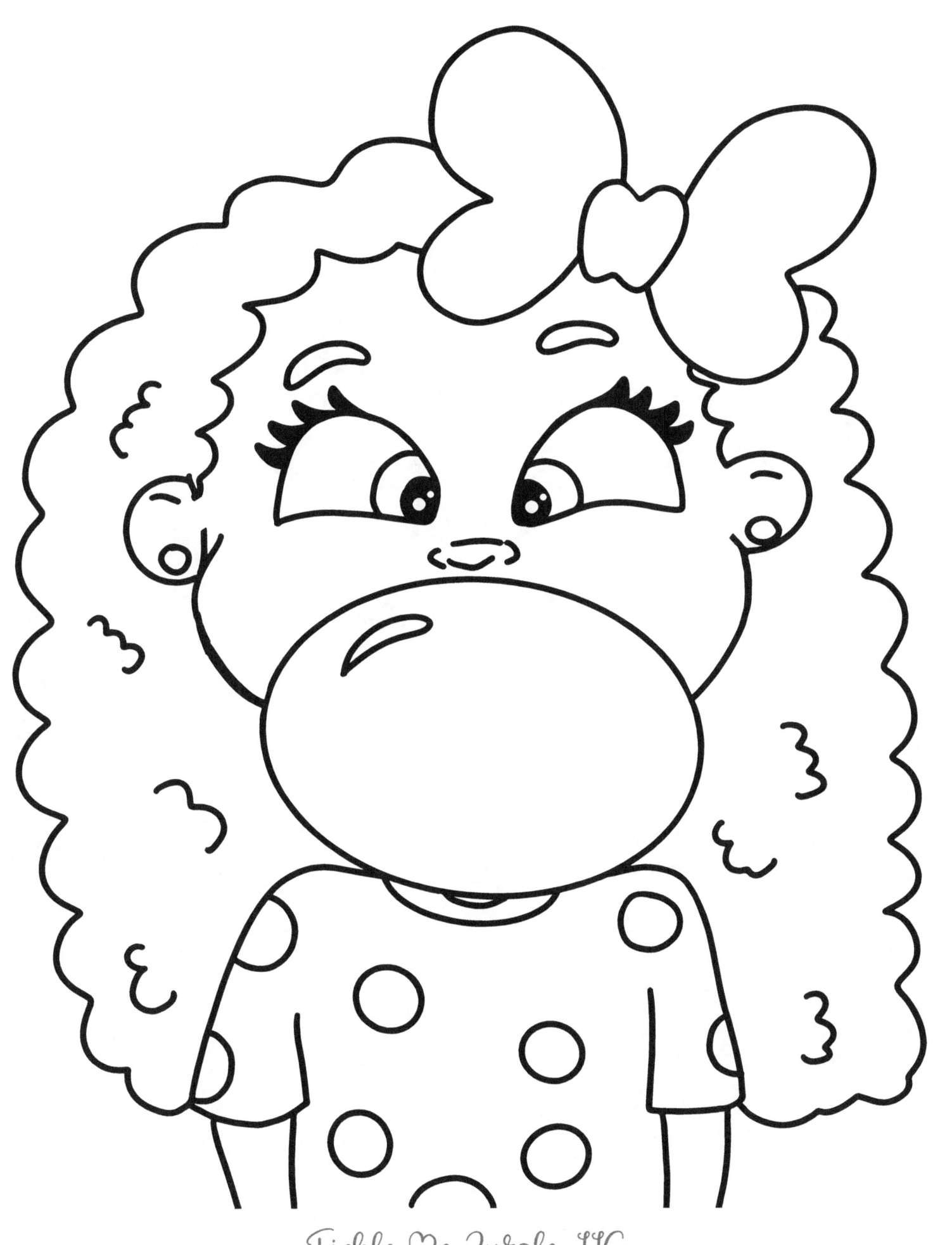

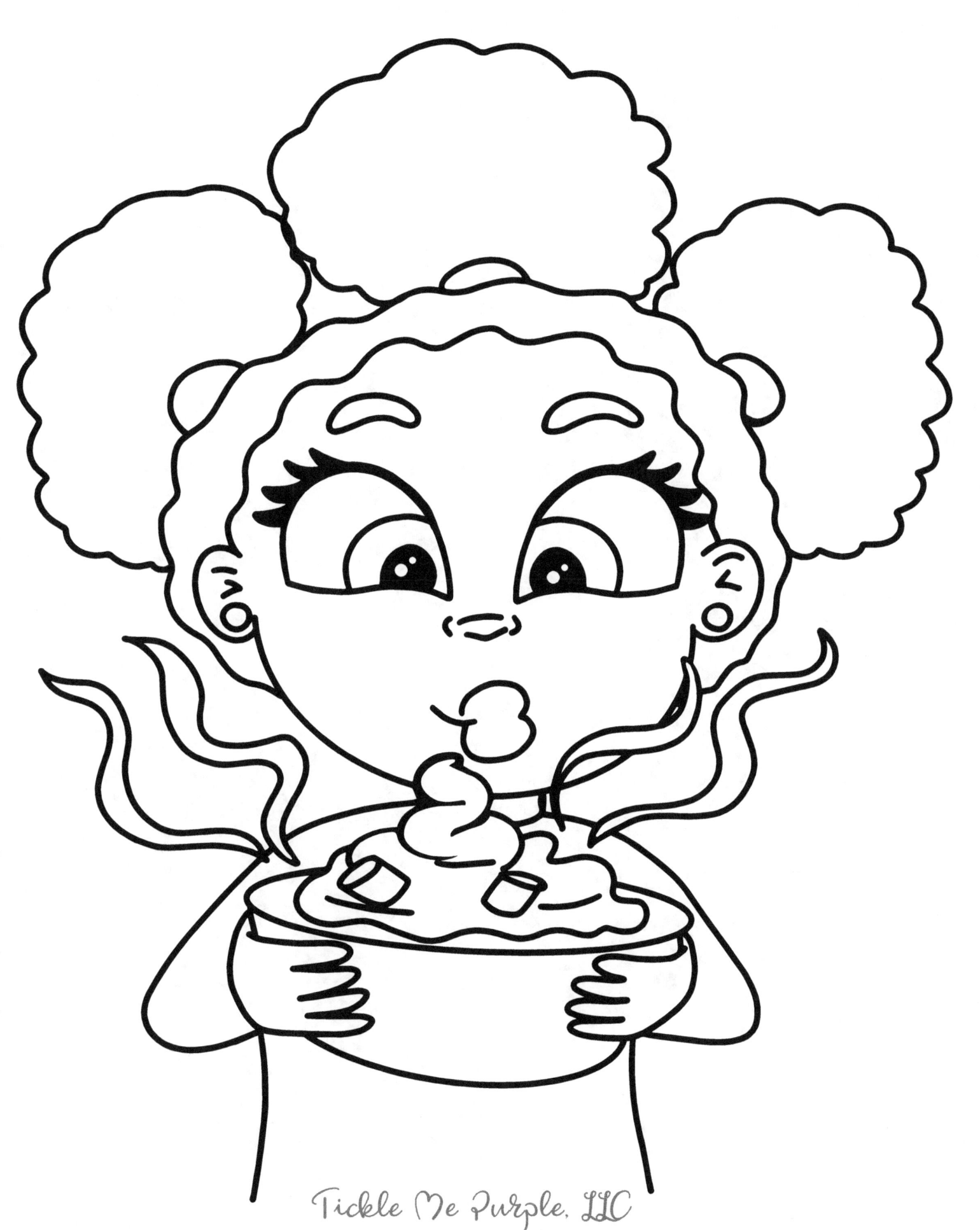

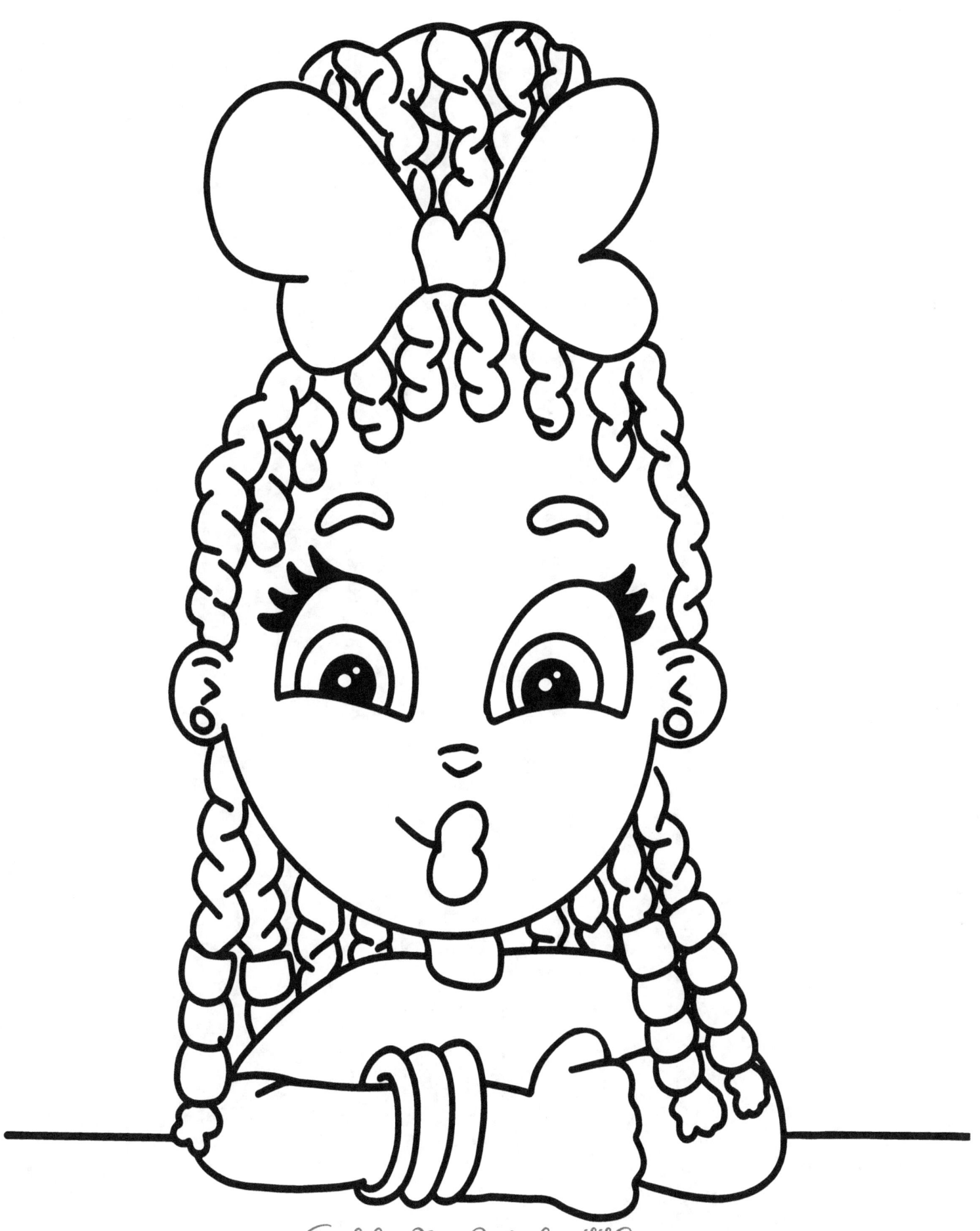

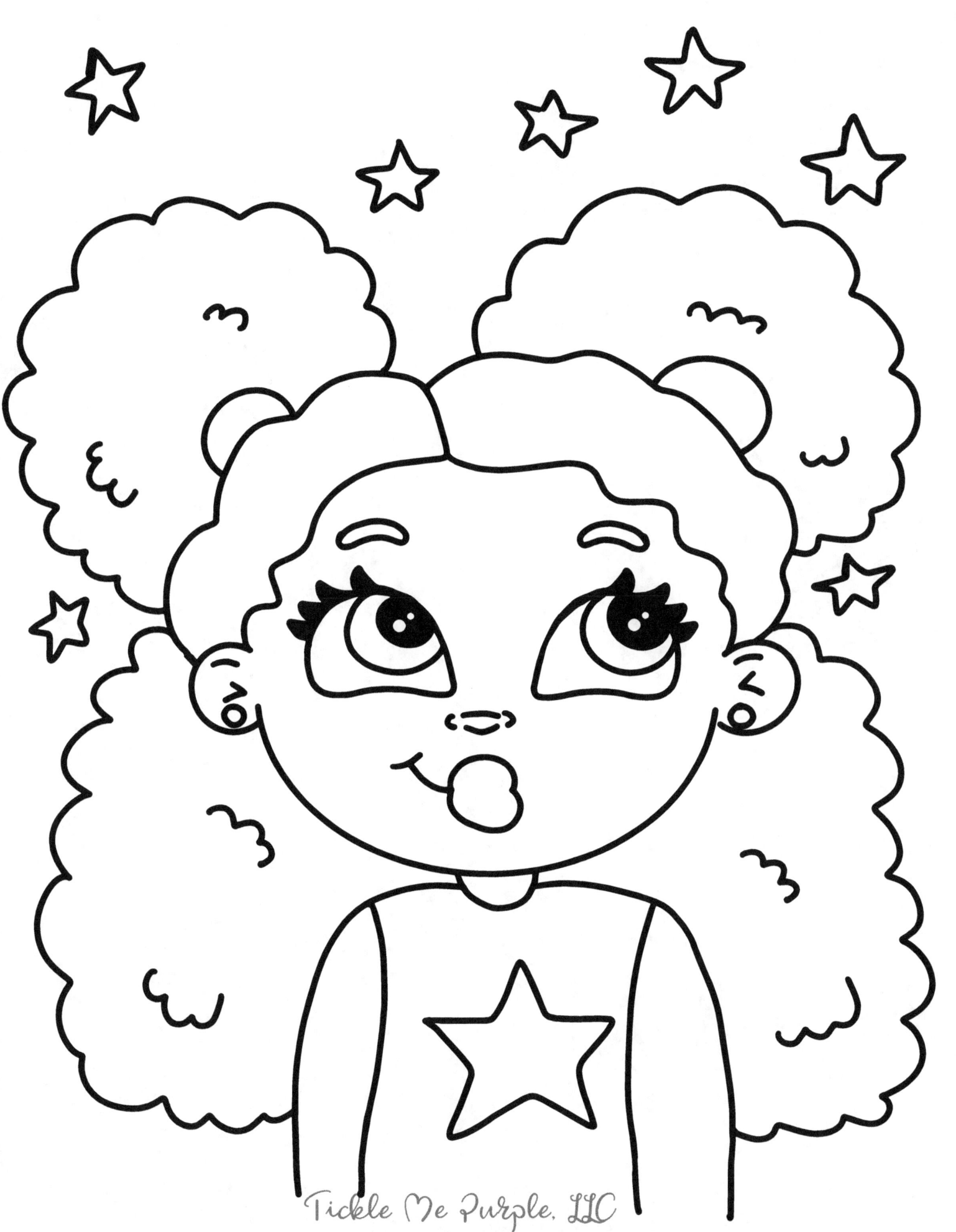

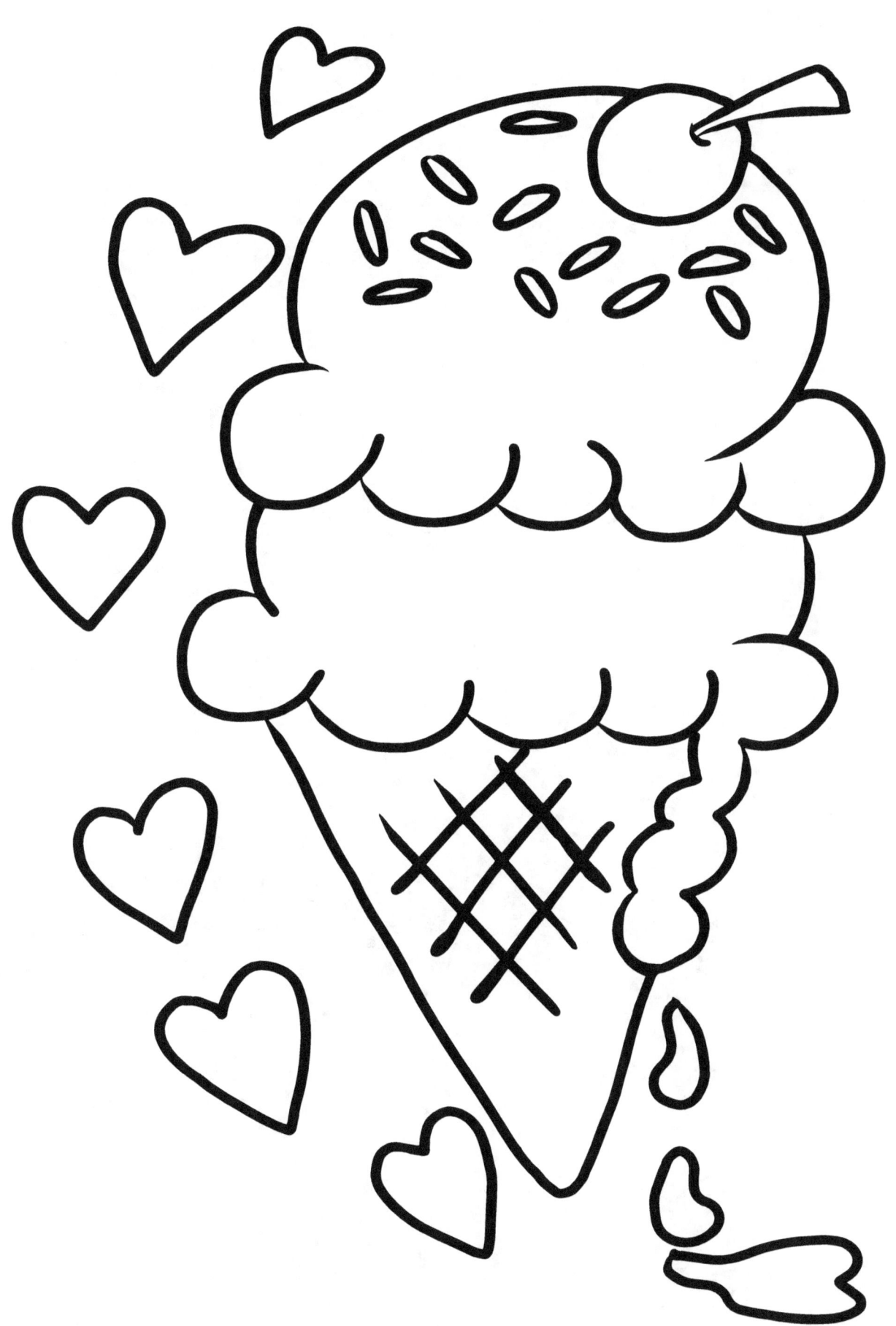

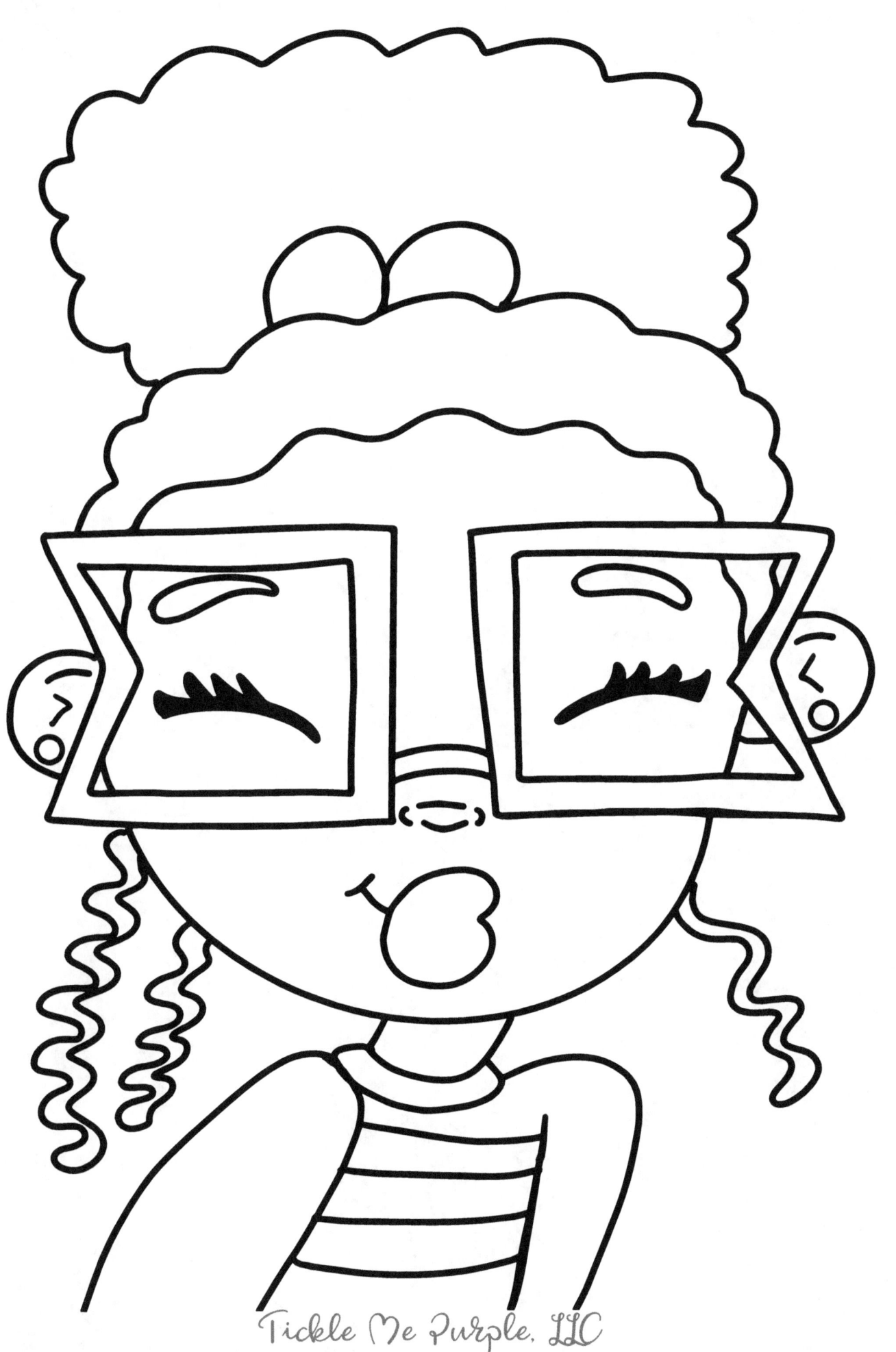

Tickle Me Purple, LLC

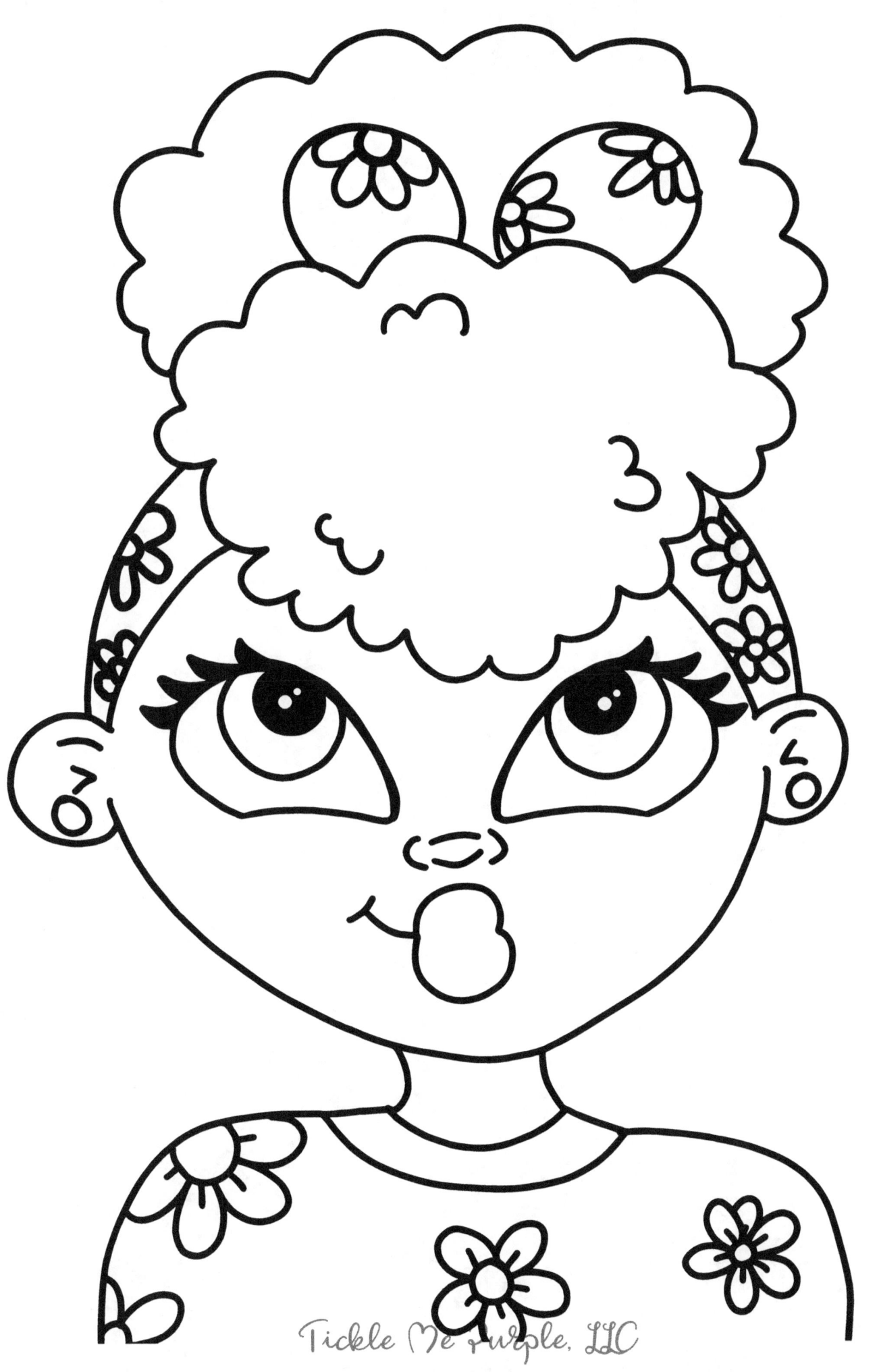

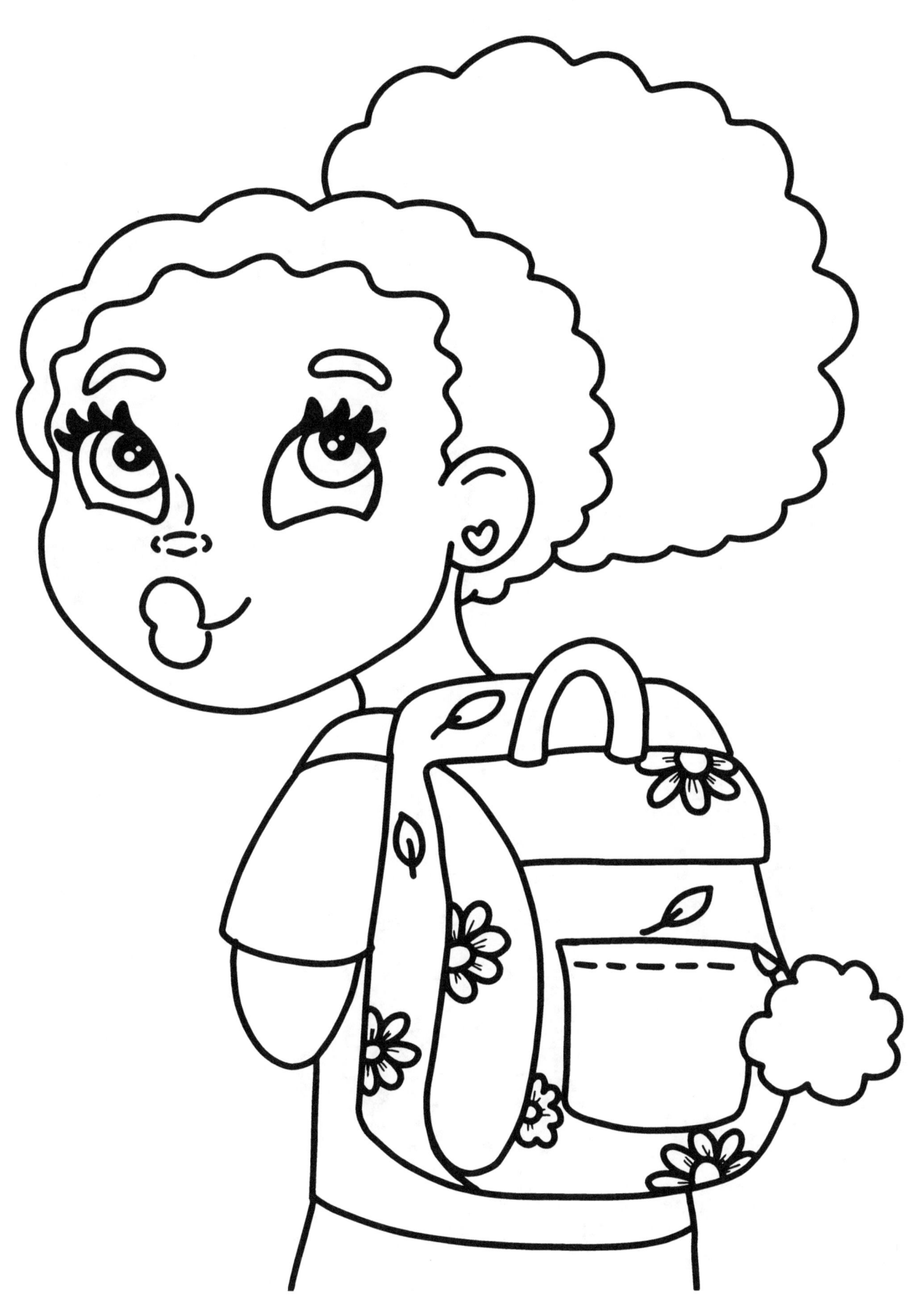

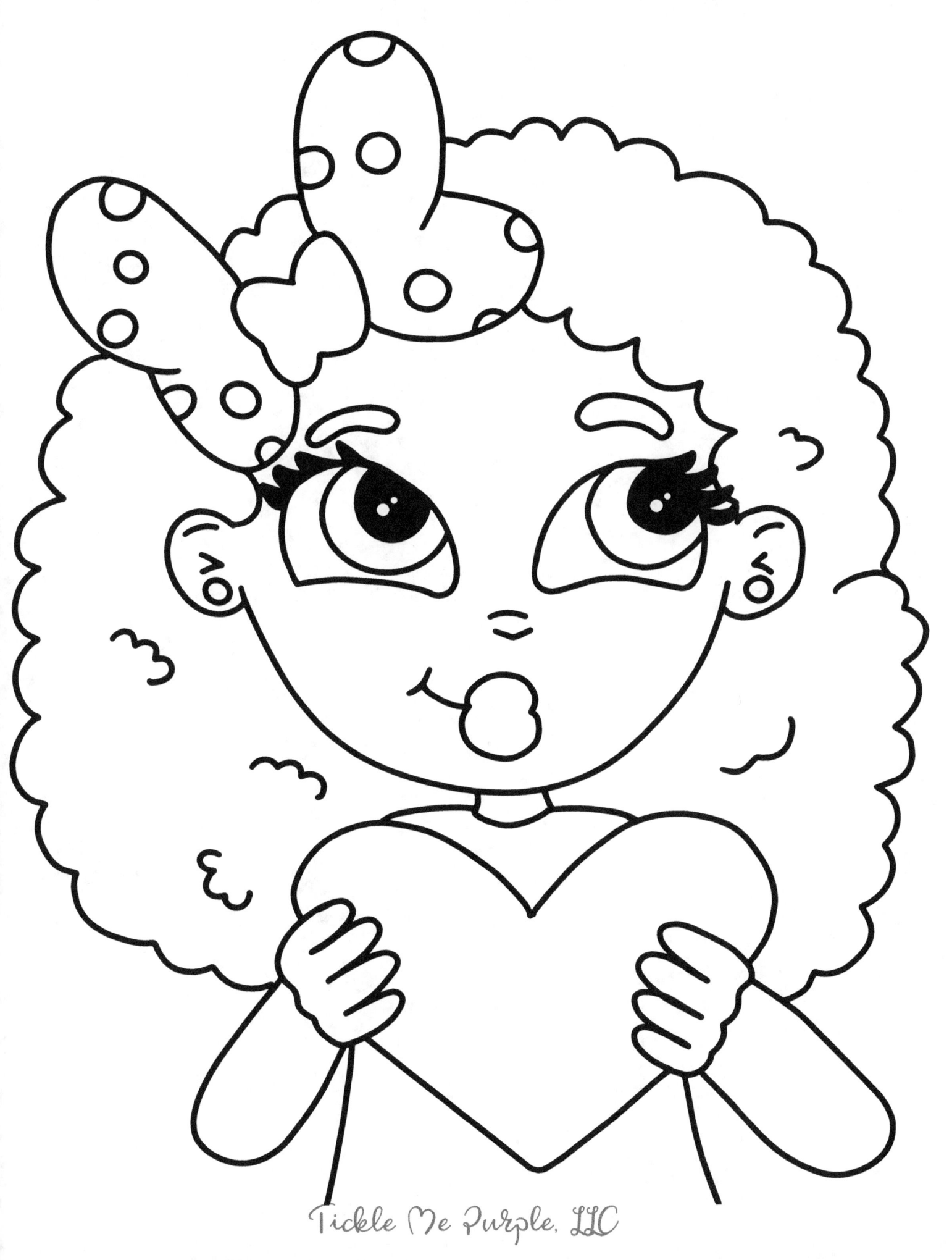

Tickle Me Purple, LLC

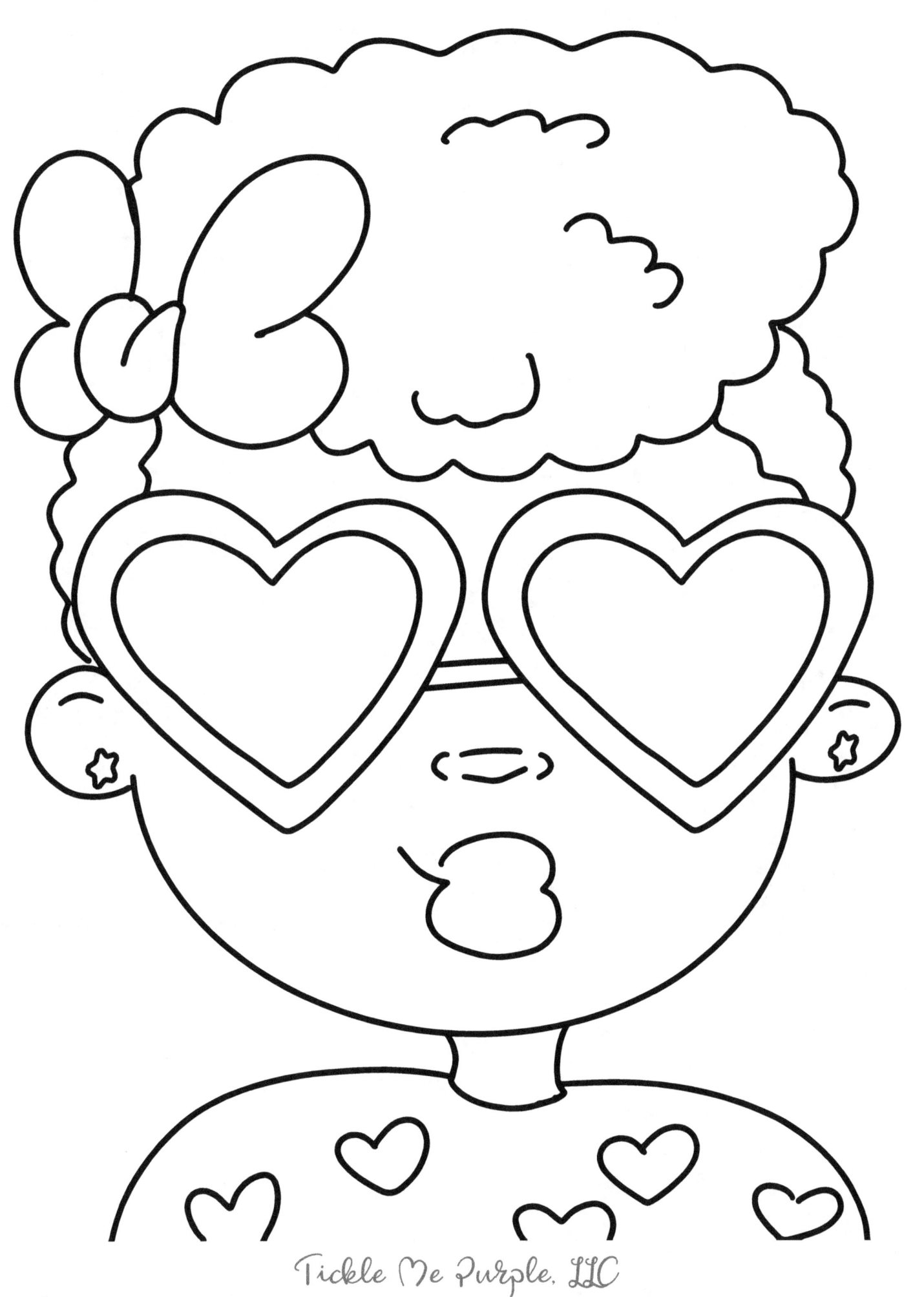

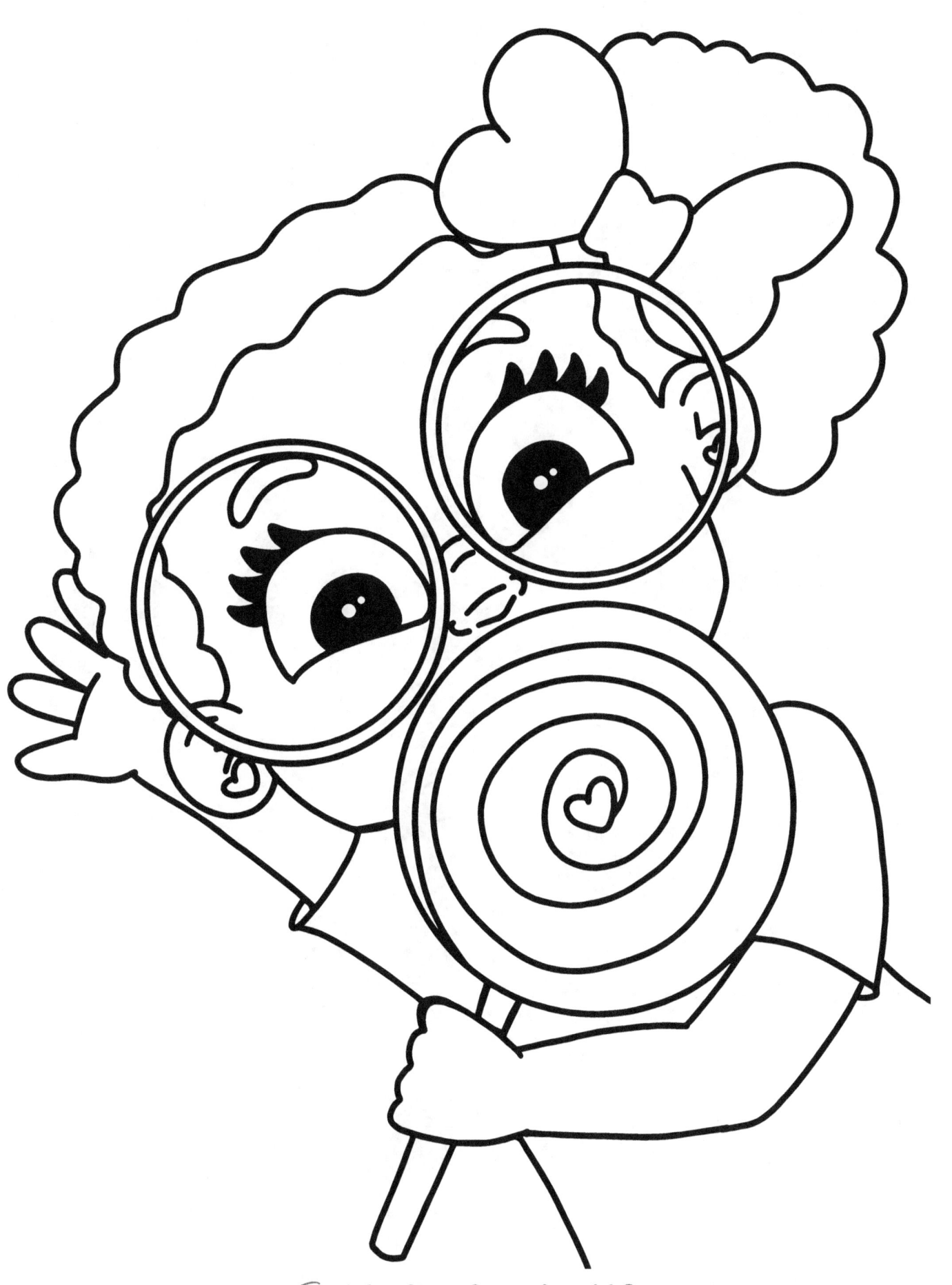

Tickle Me Purple, LLC

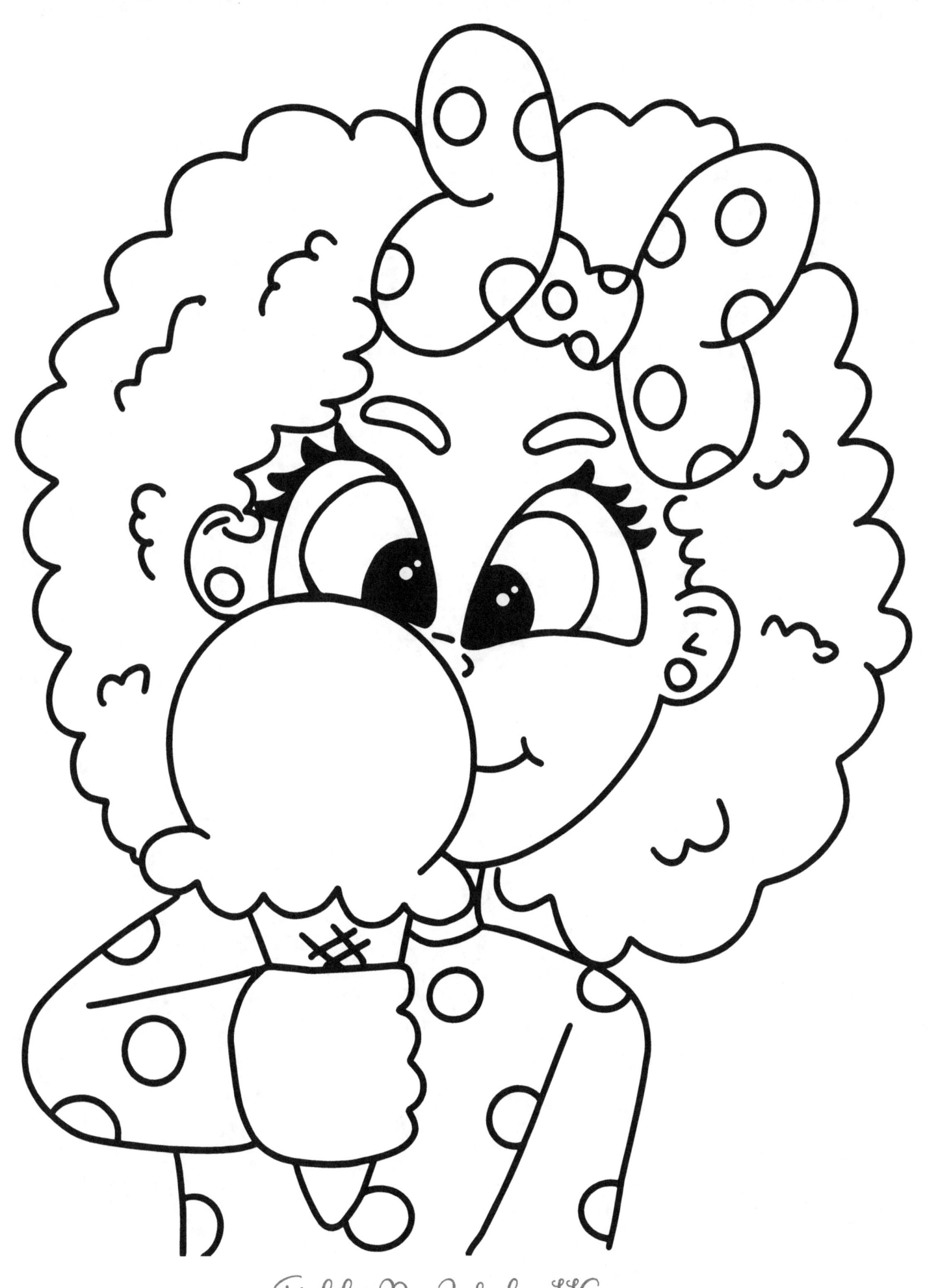

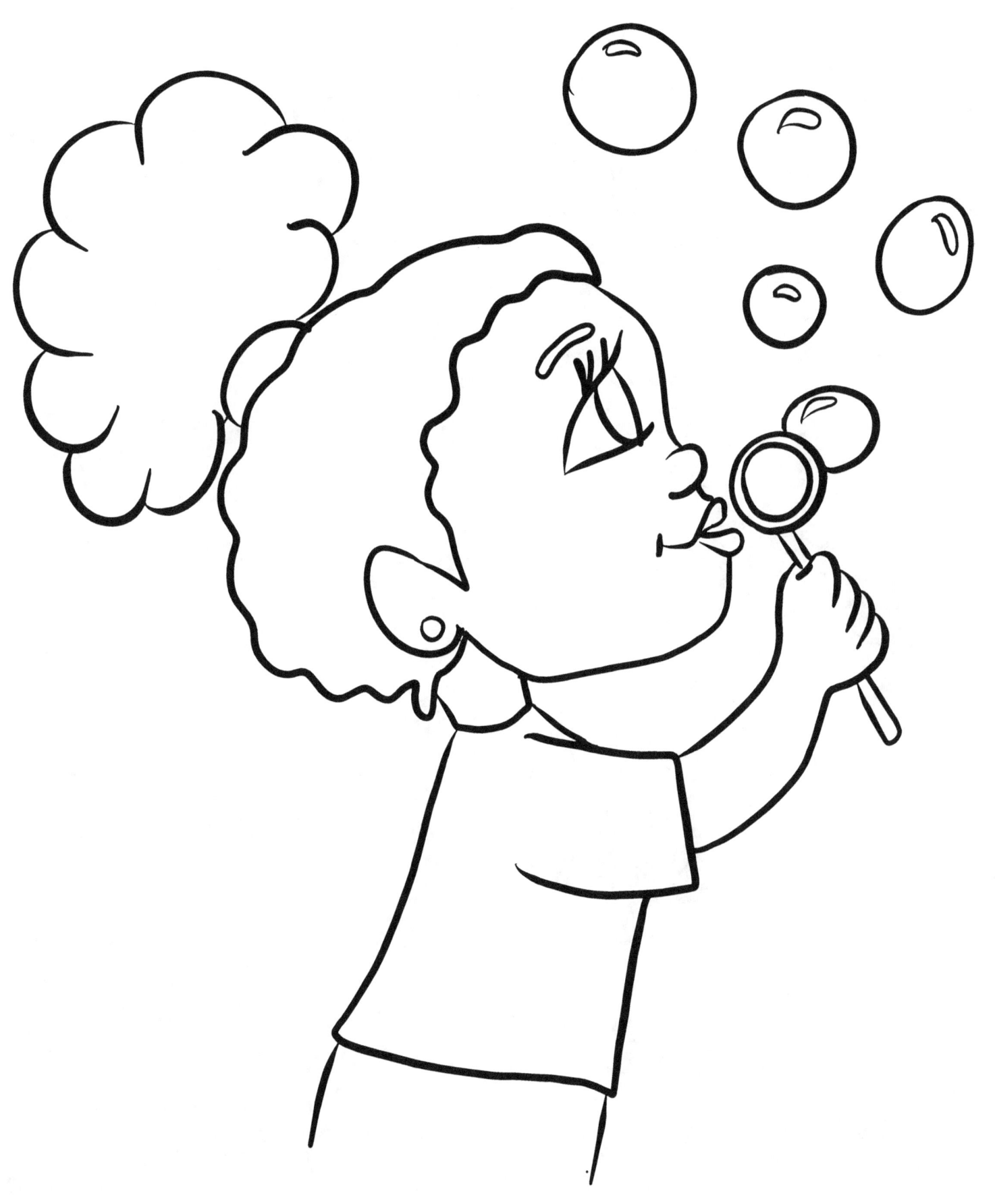

Tickle Me Purple, LLC

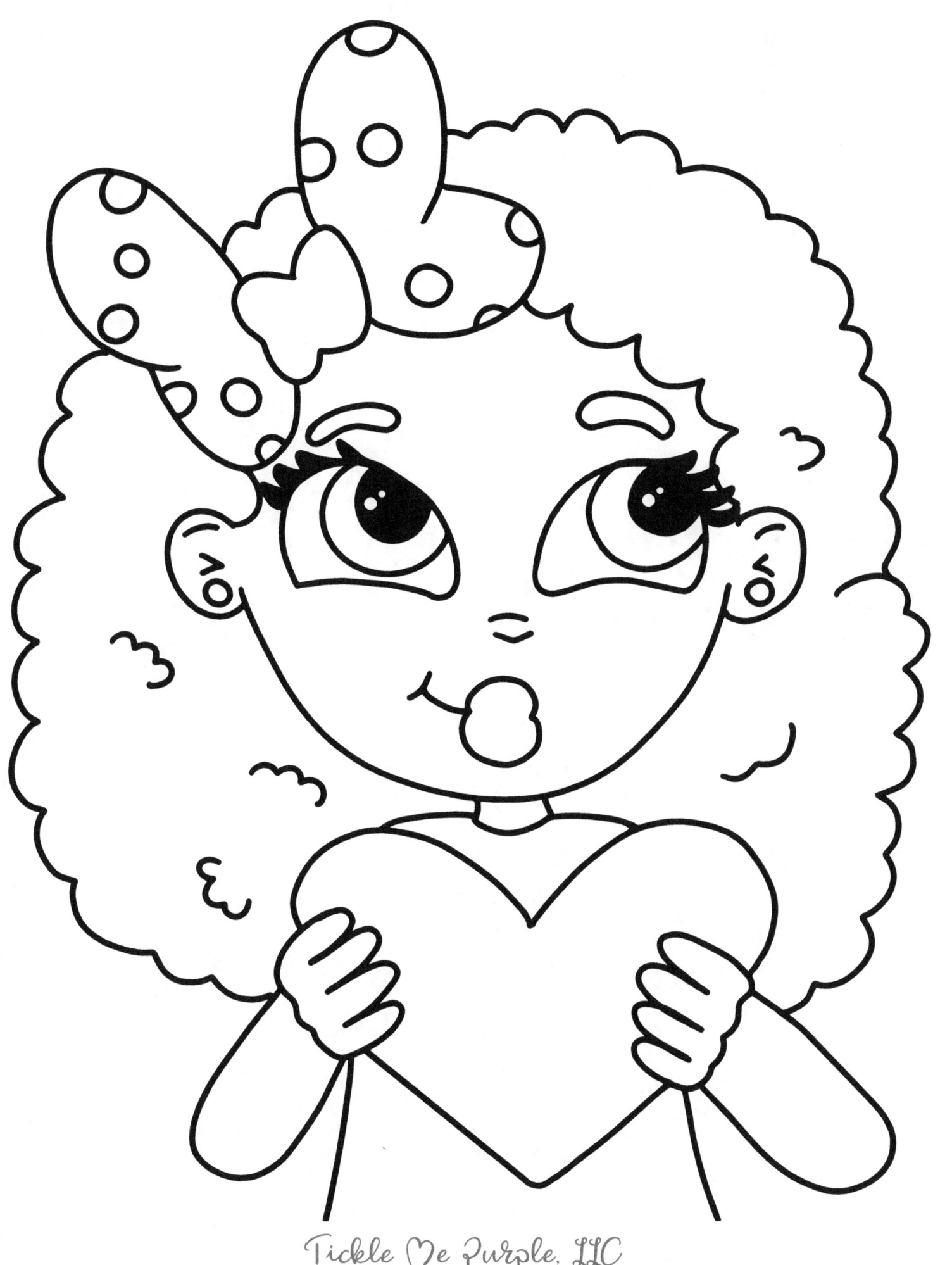

Tickle Me Purple, LLC

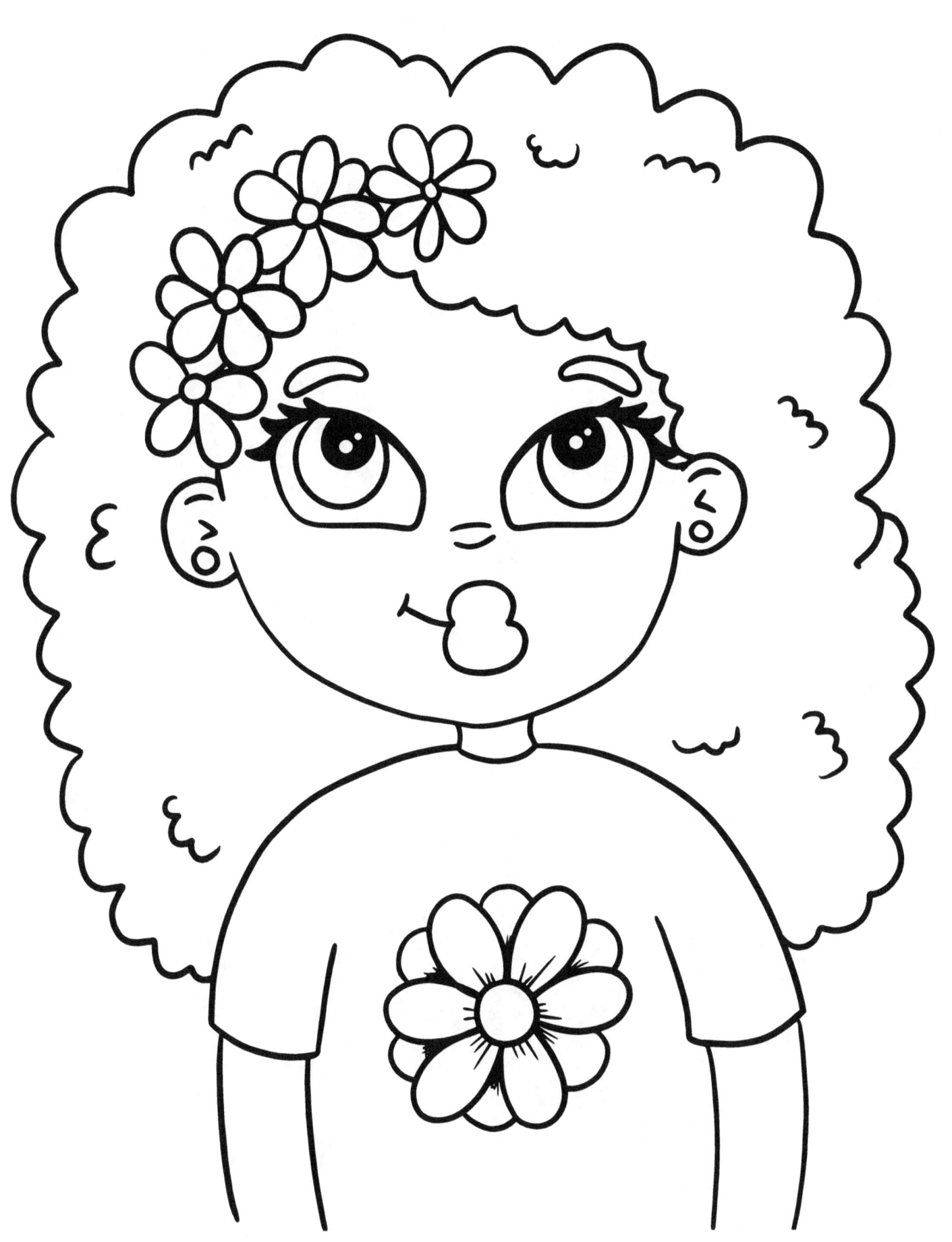

Tickle Me Purple, LLC

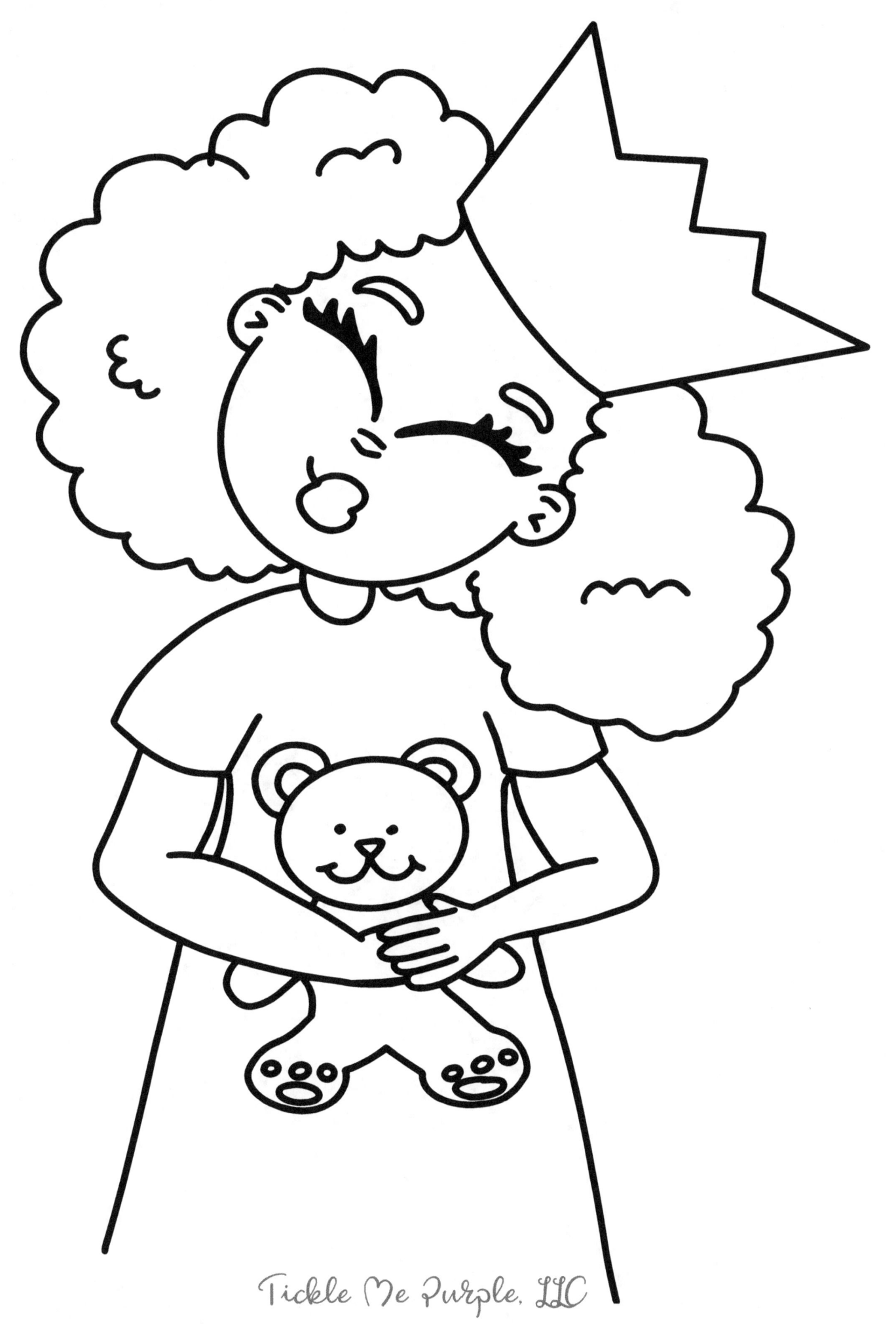

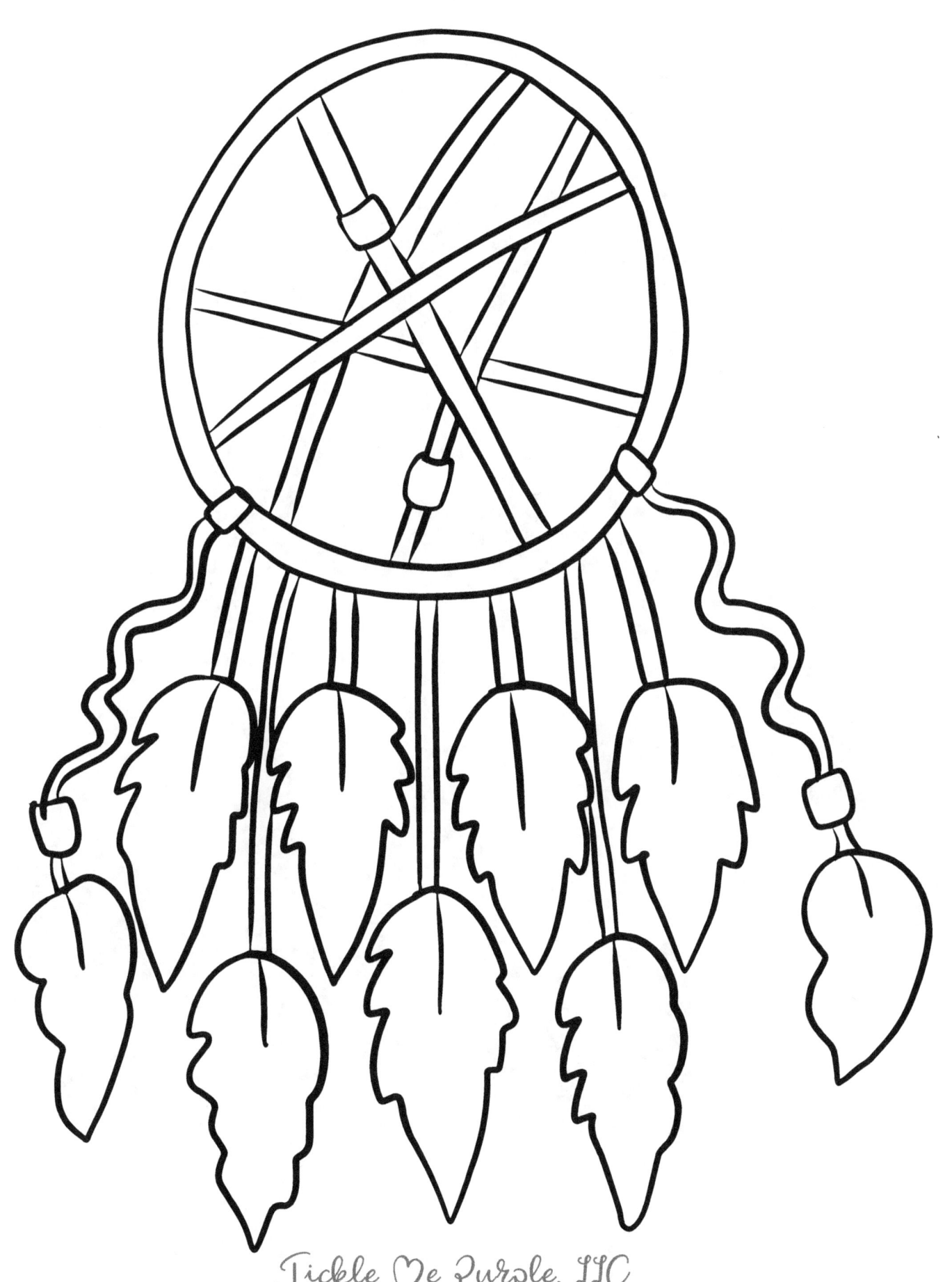

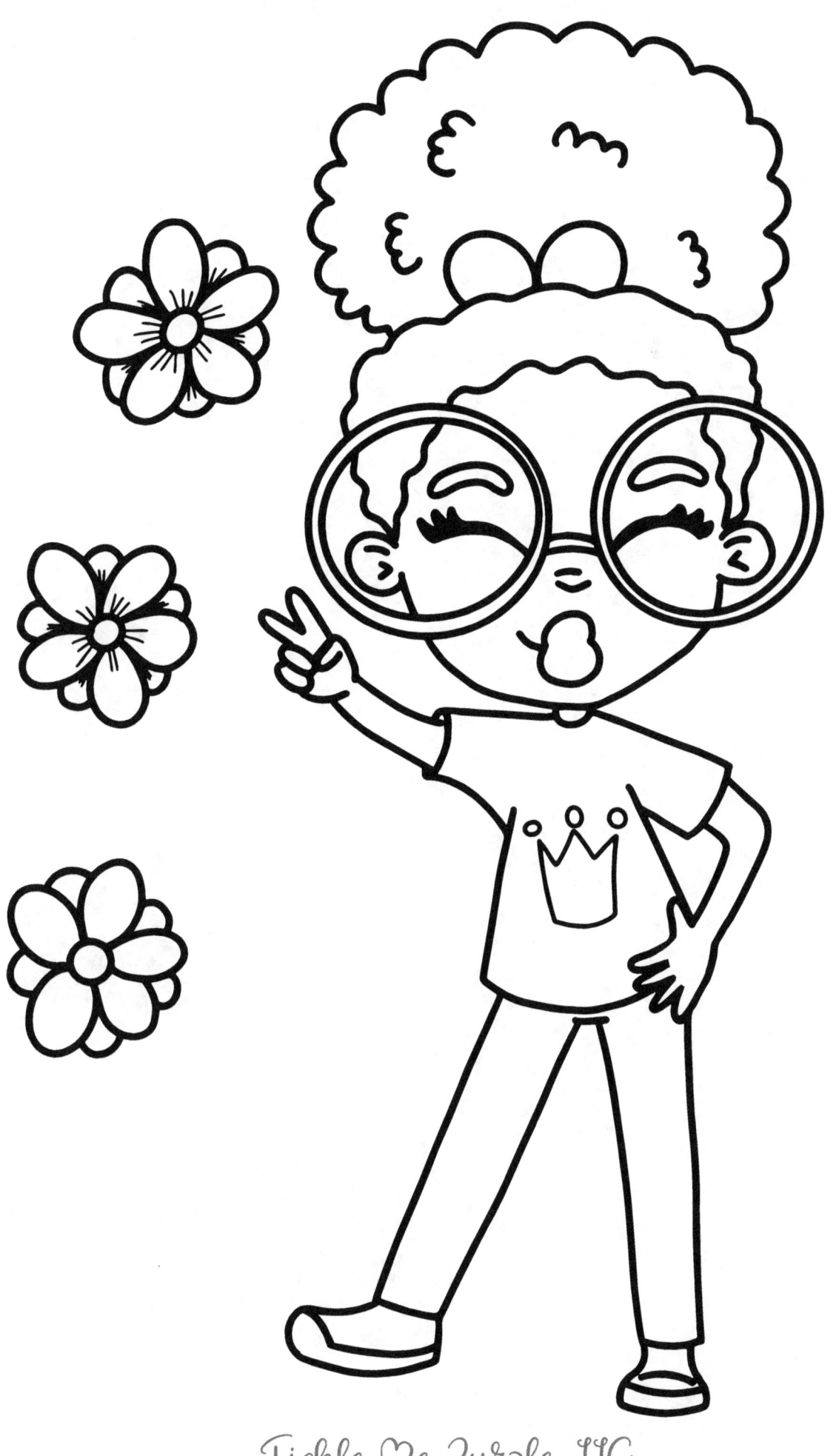

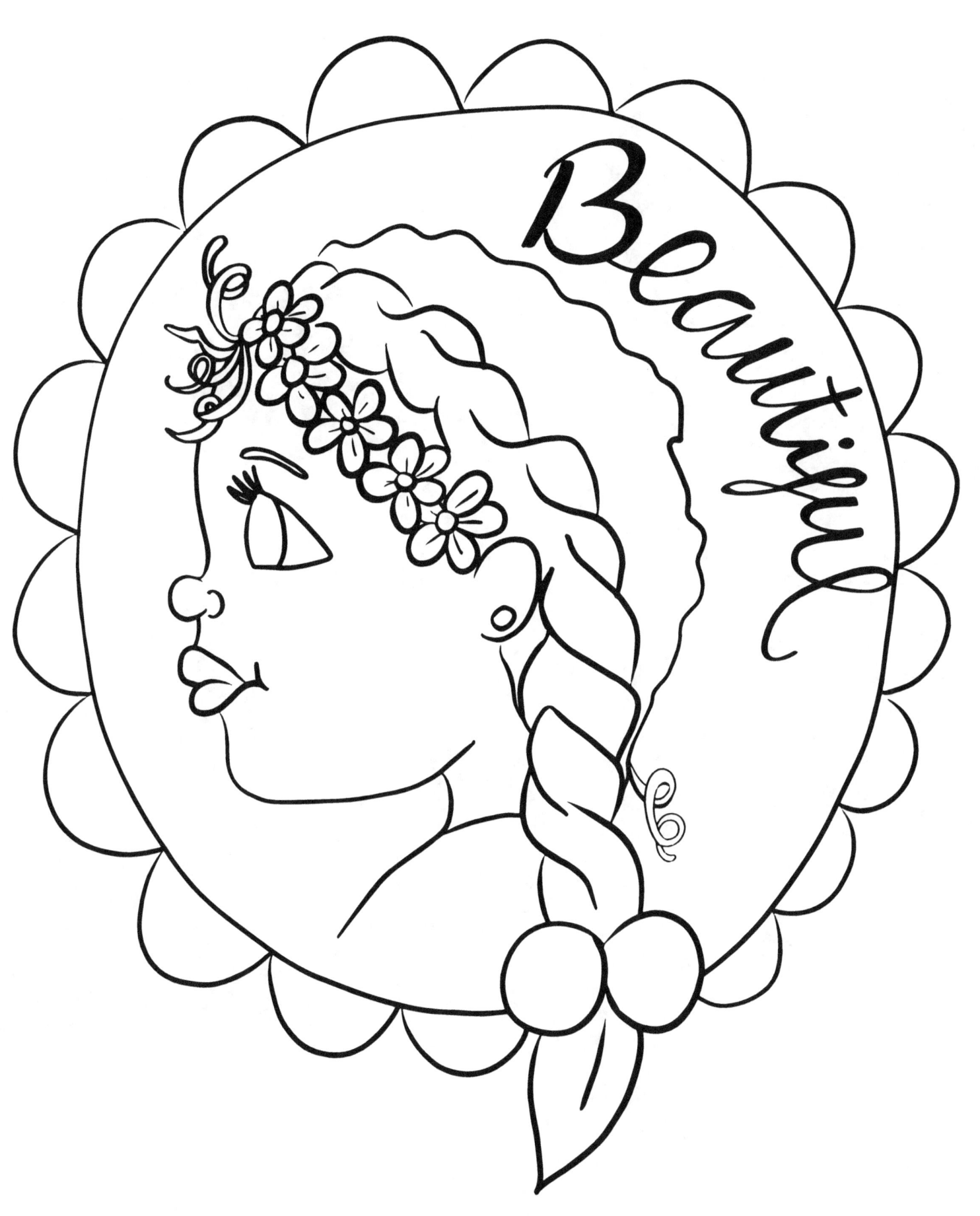

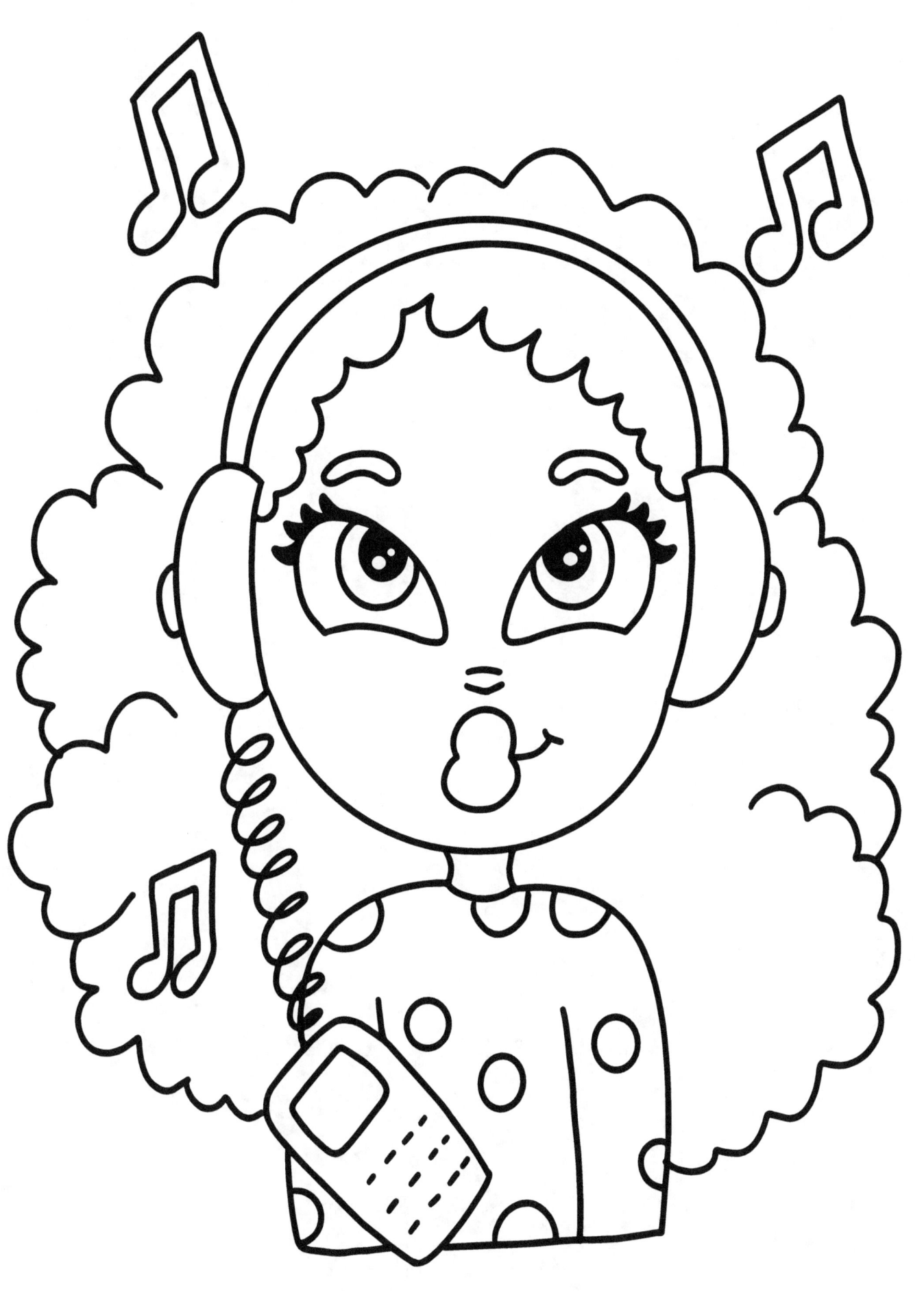

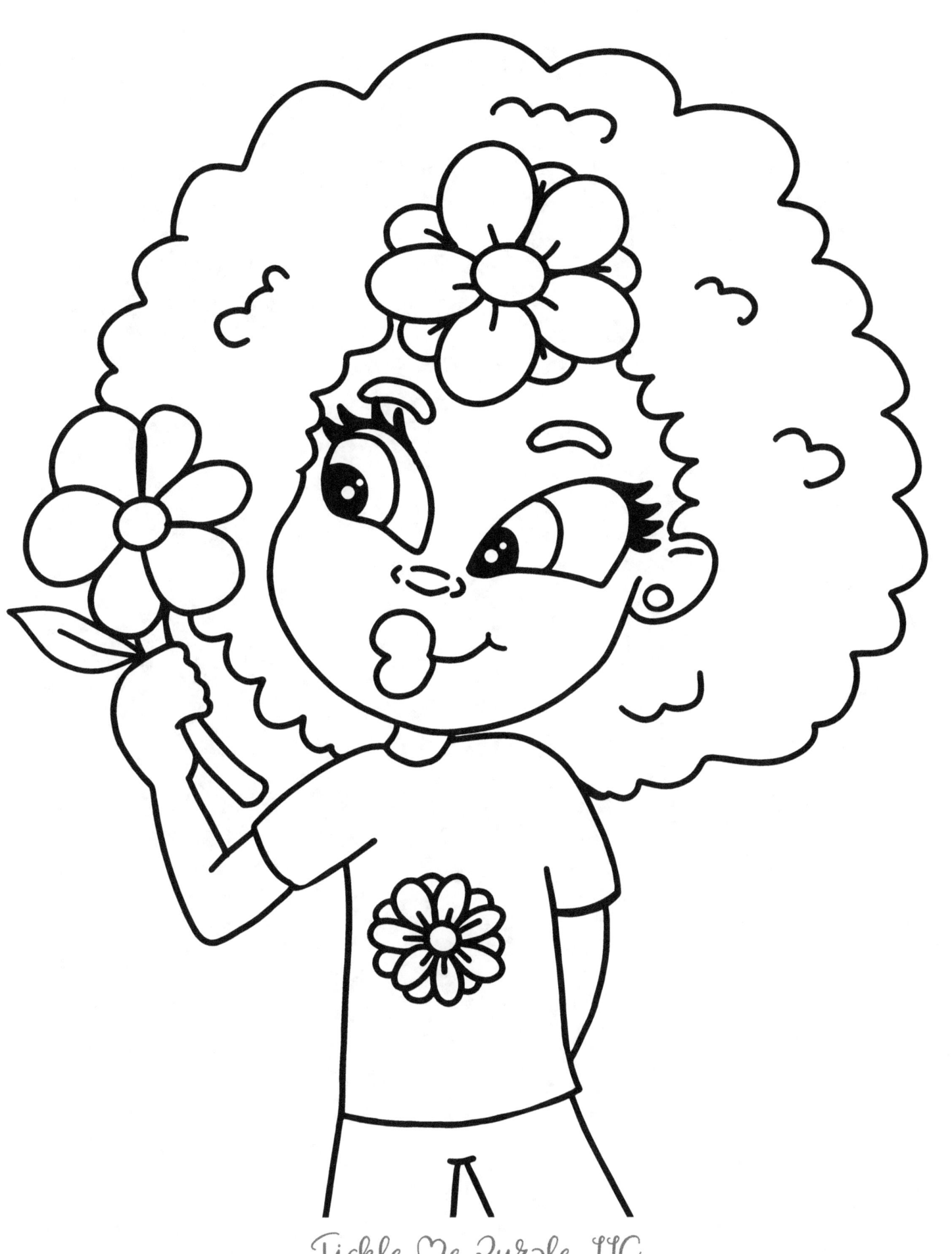

Tickle Me Purple, LLC

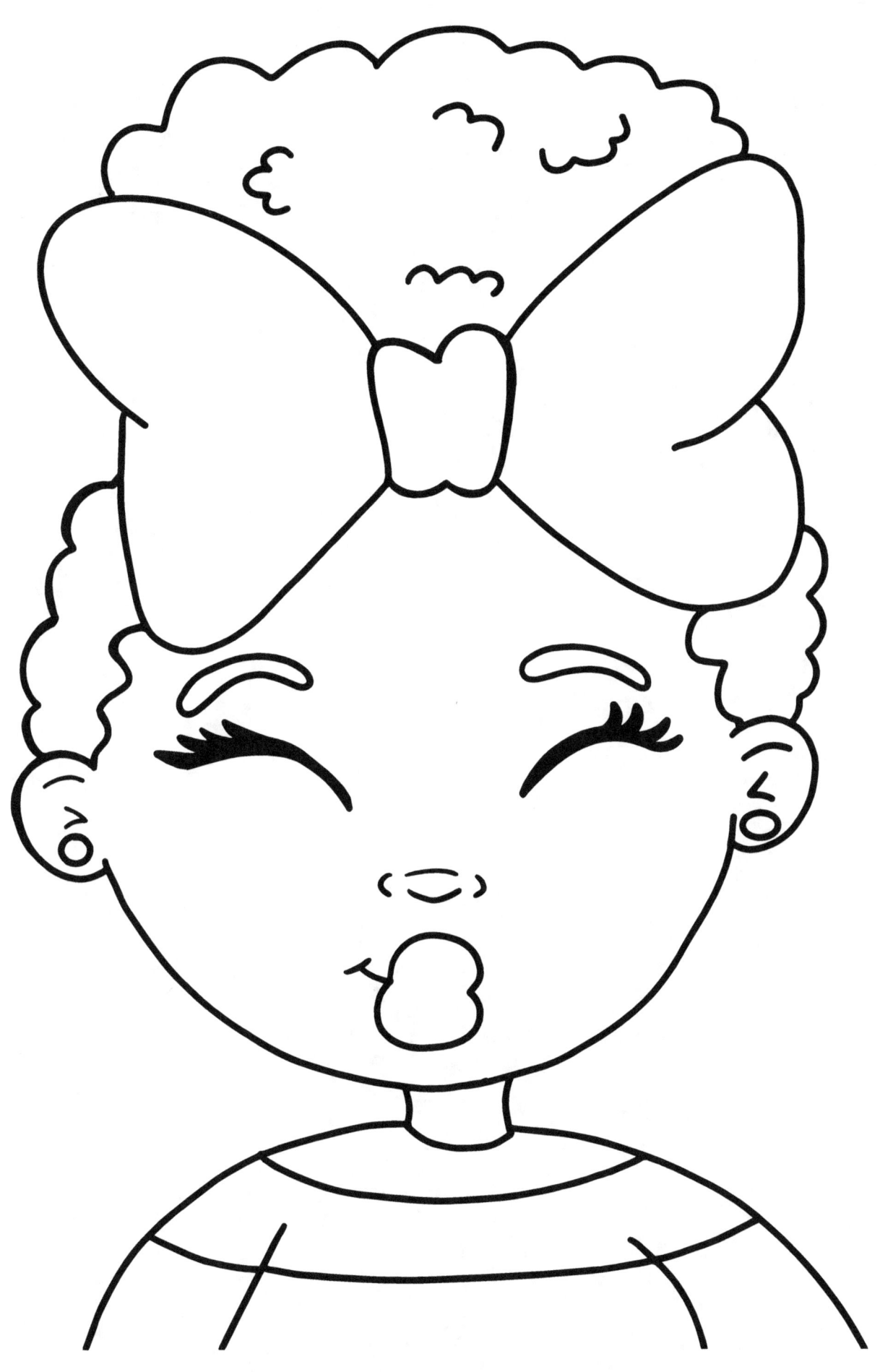

Tickle Me Purple, LLC

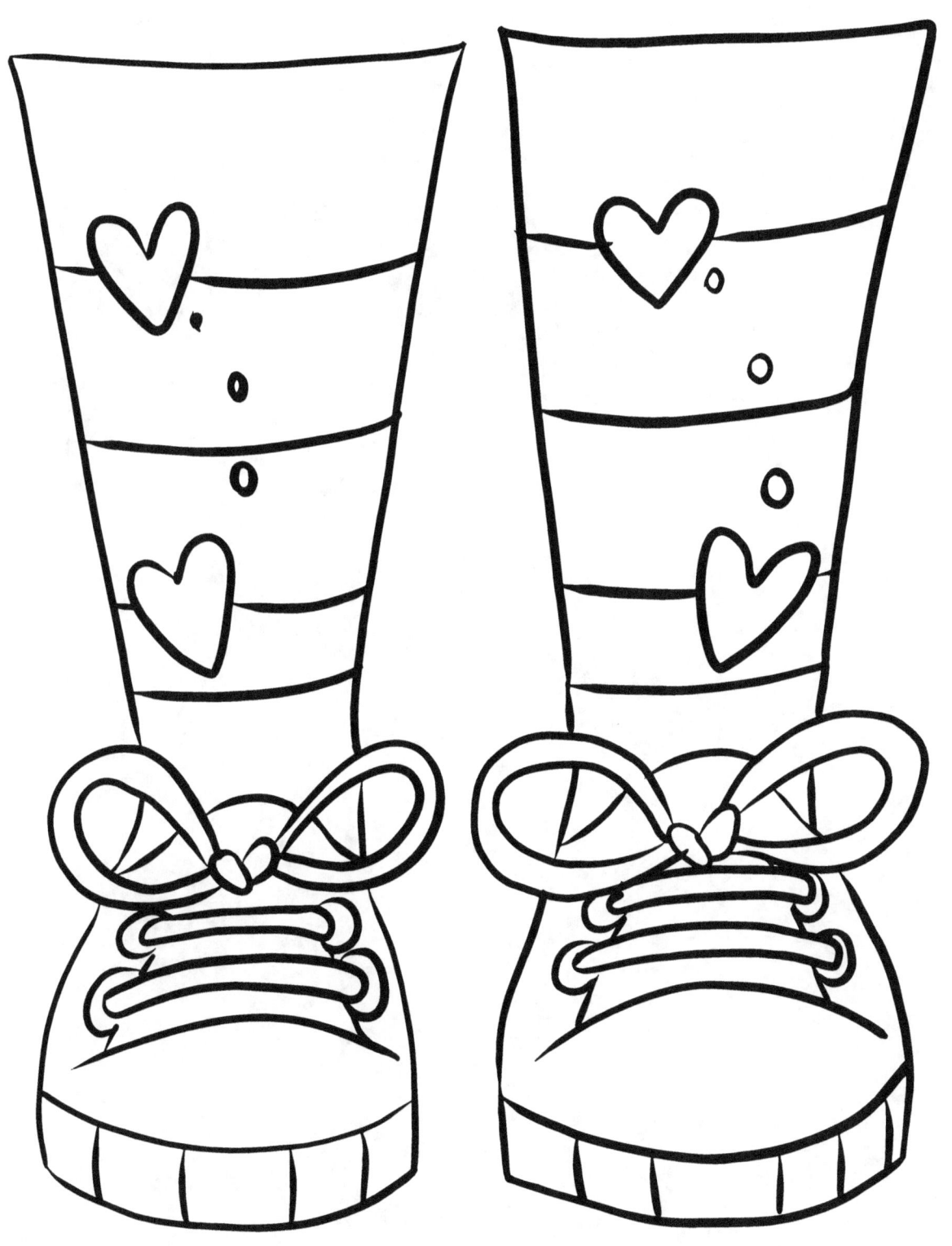

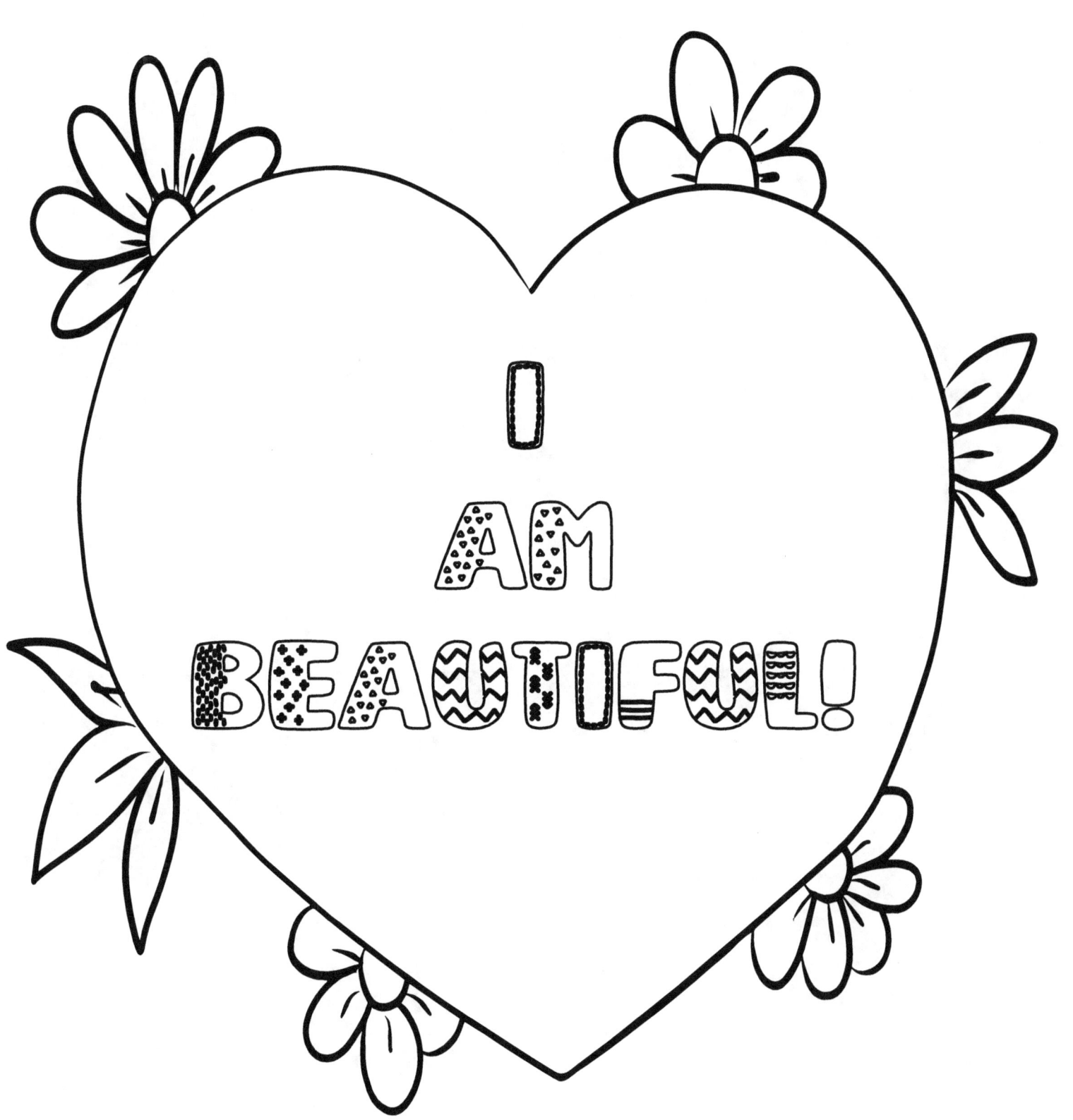

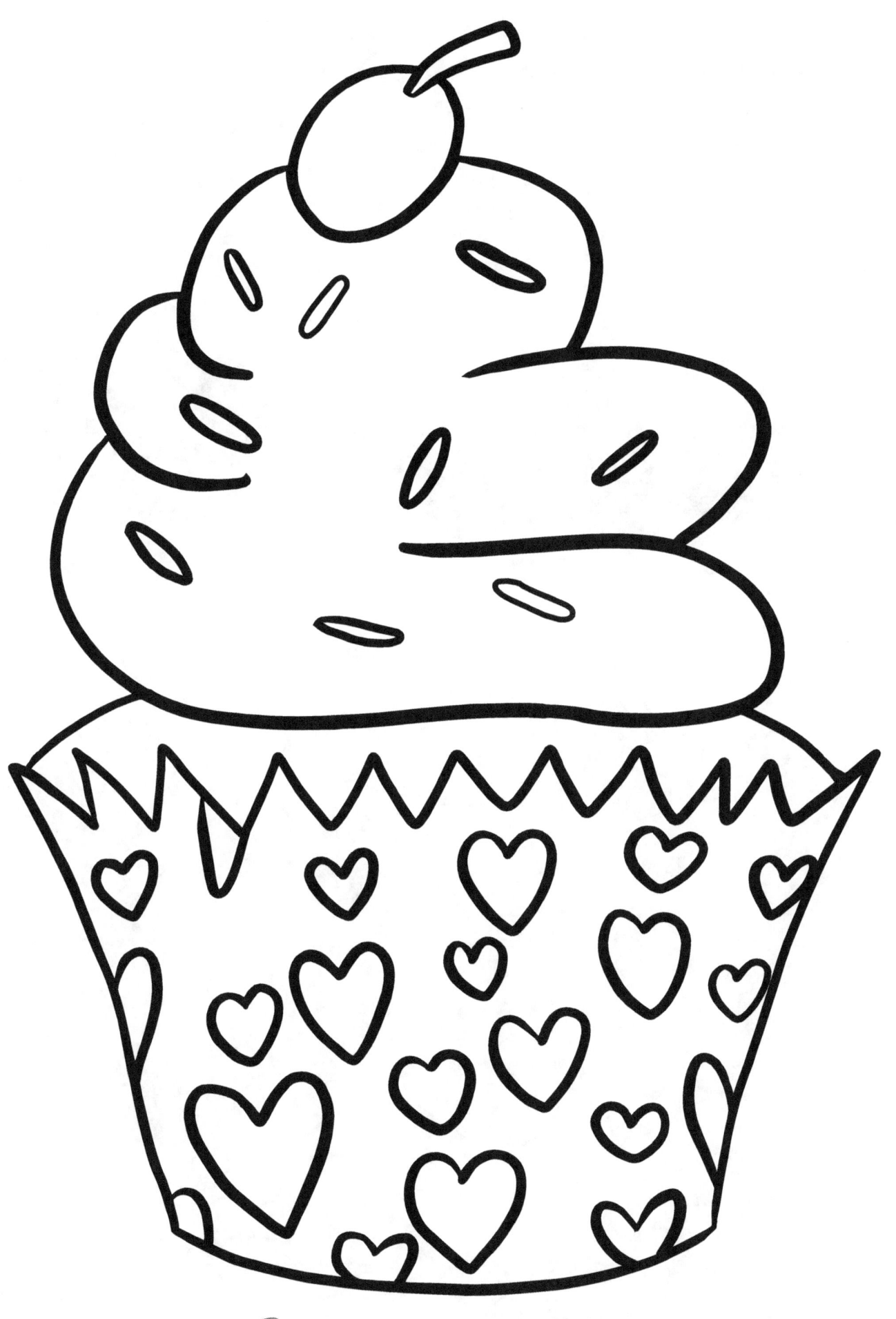

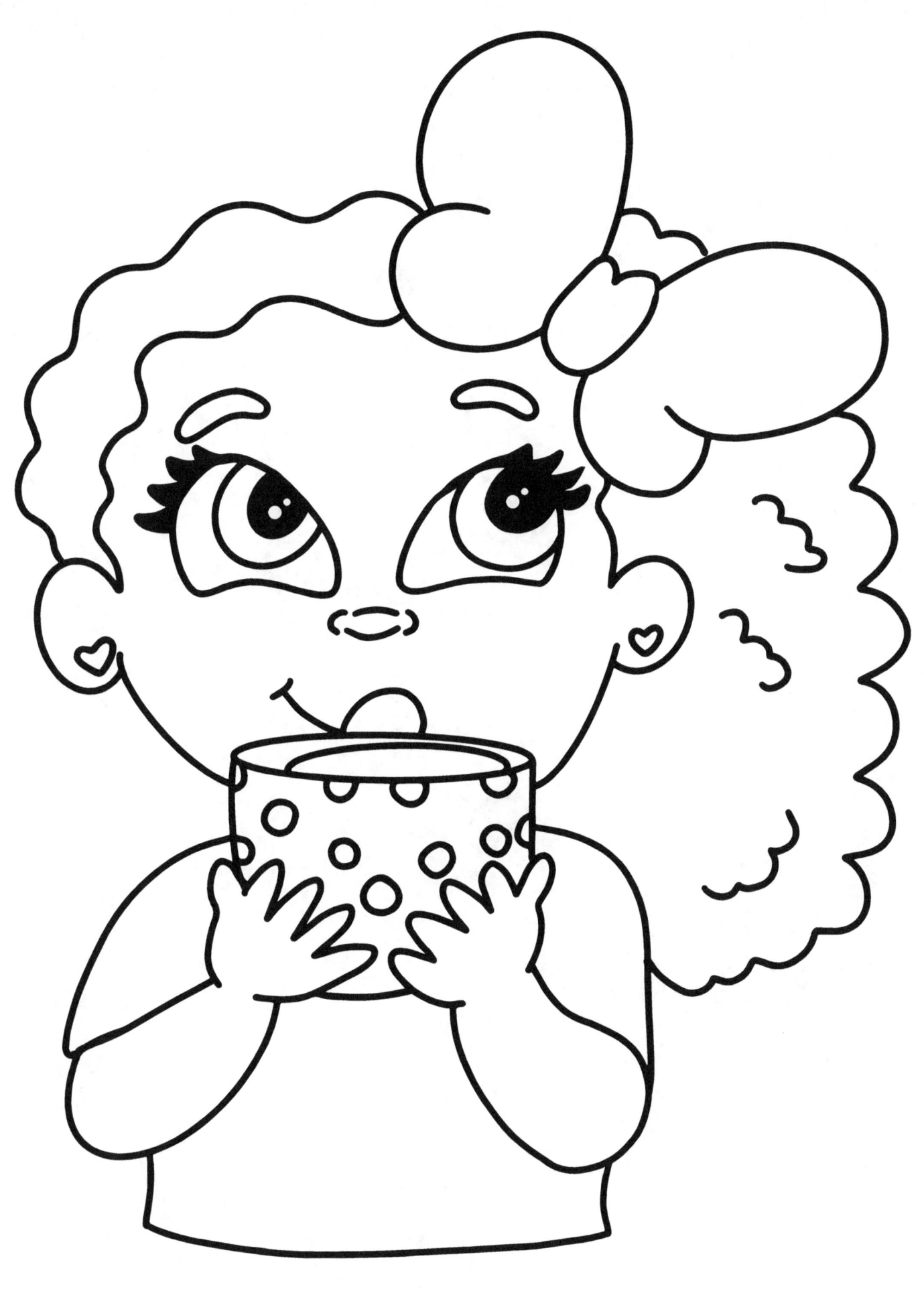

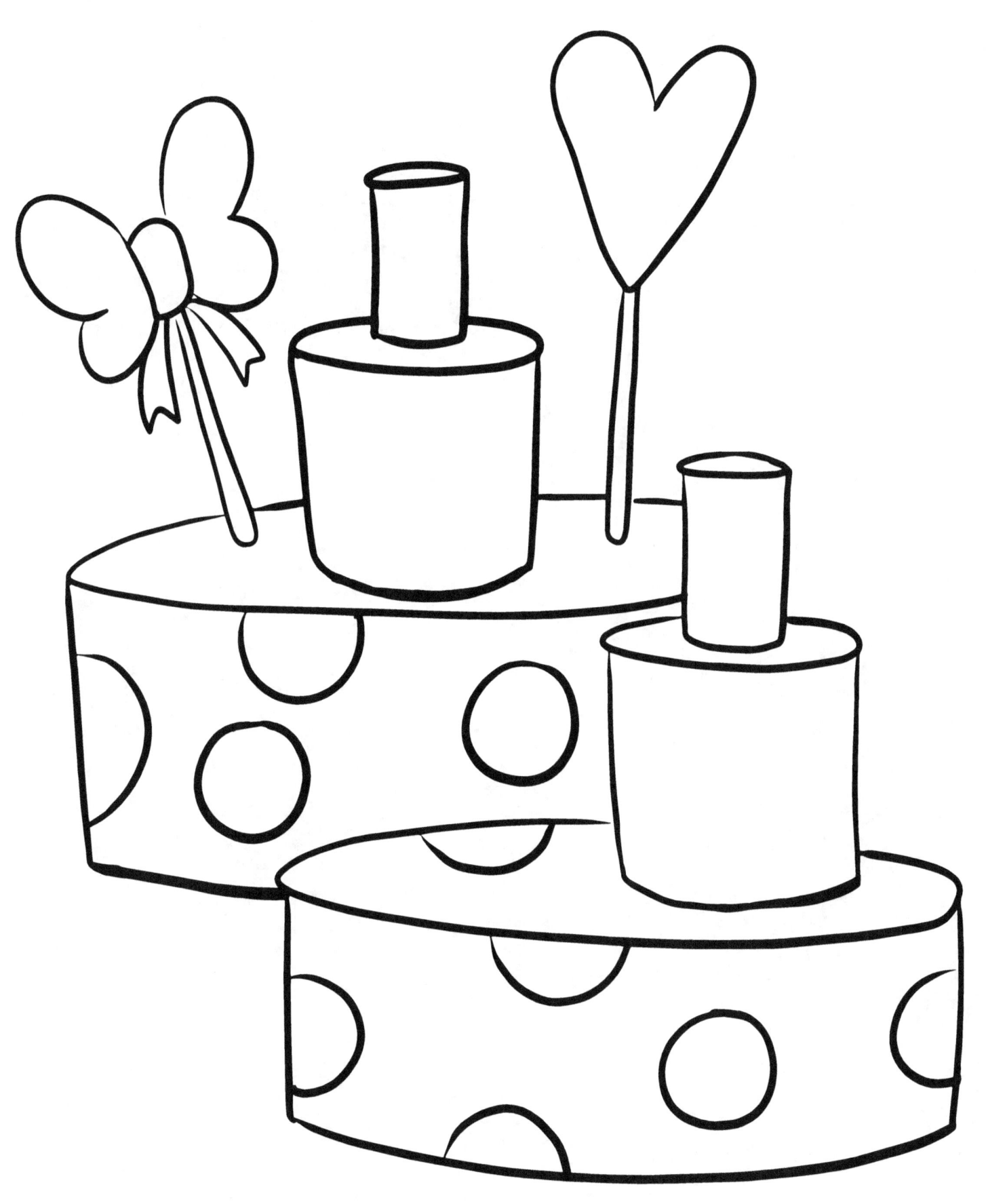

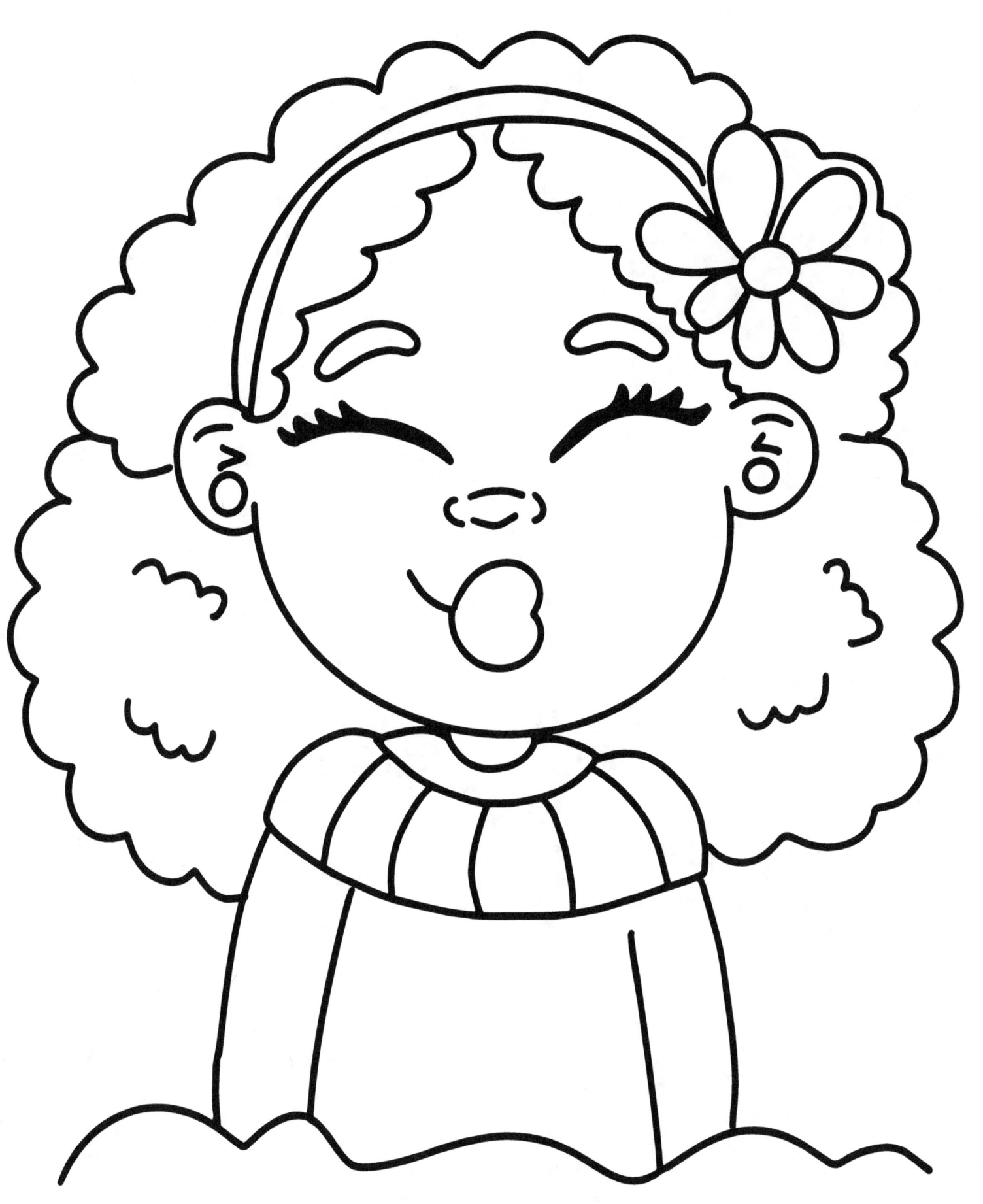

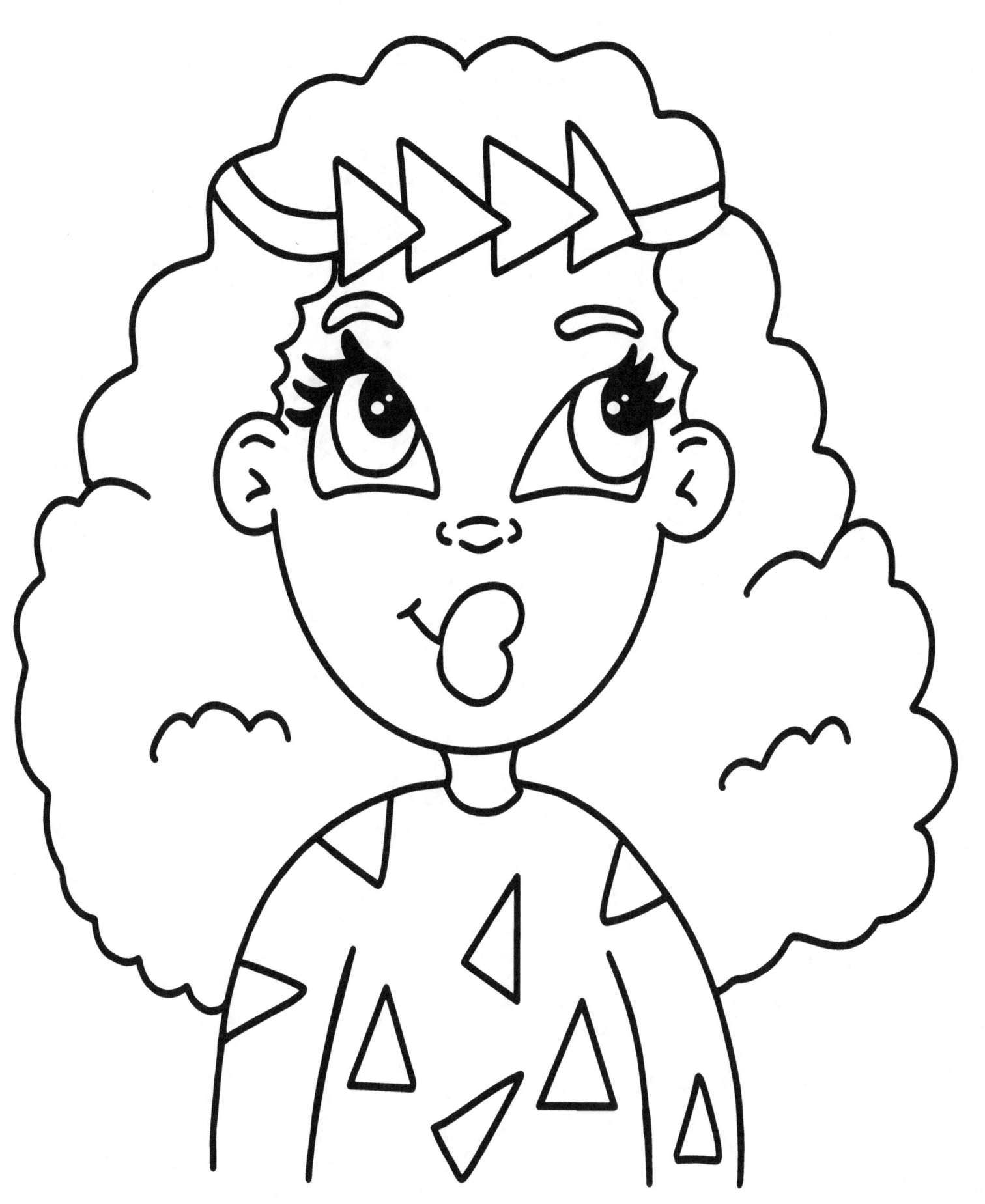

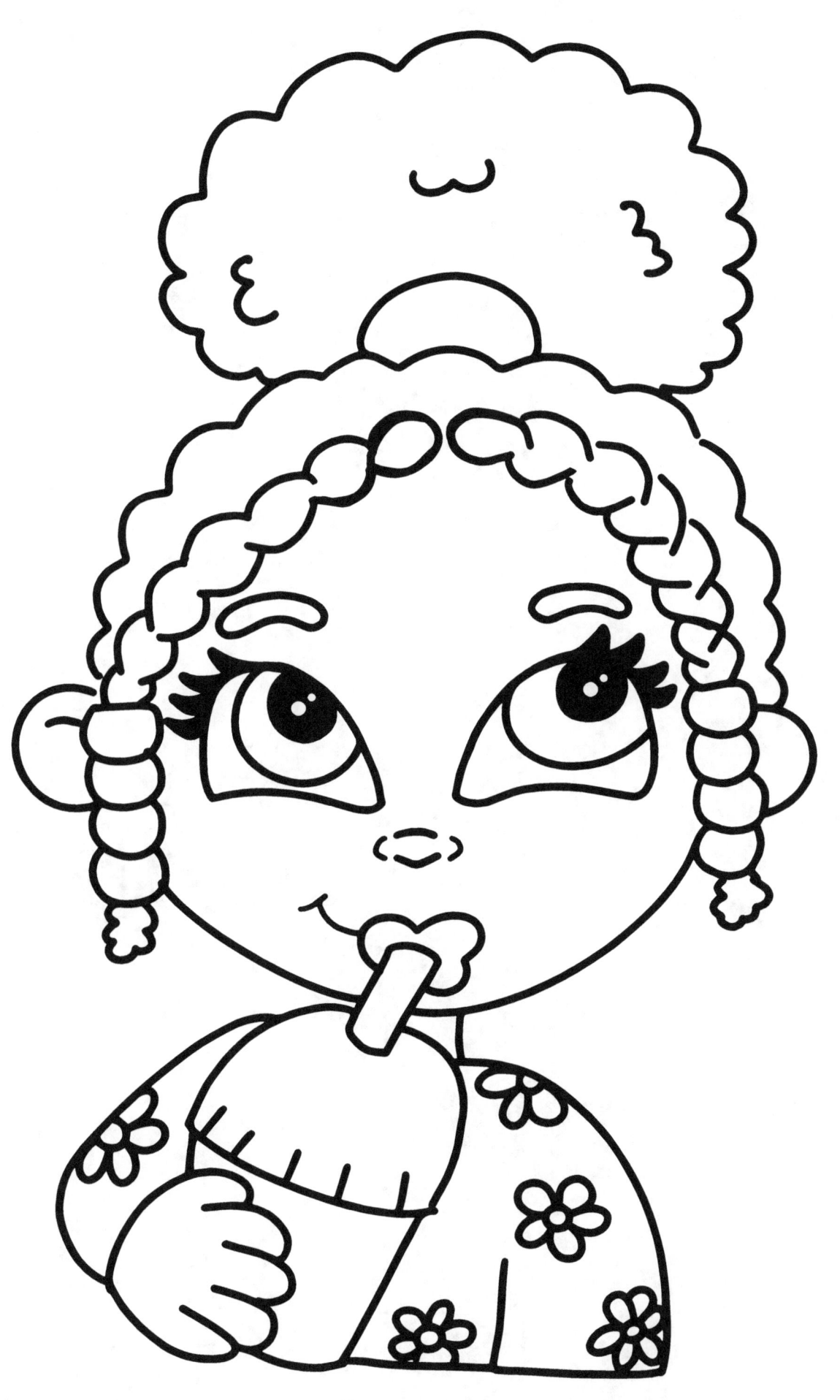

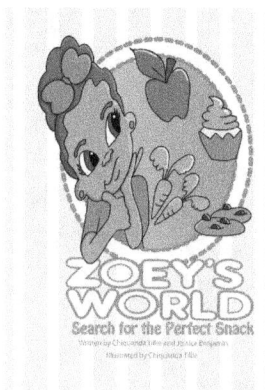
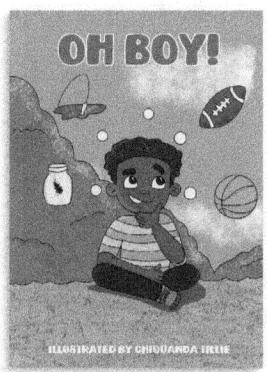
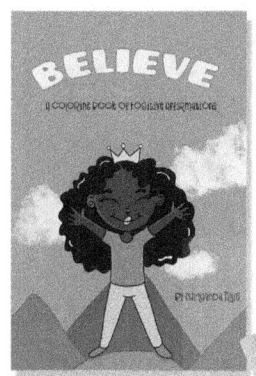
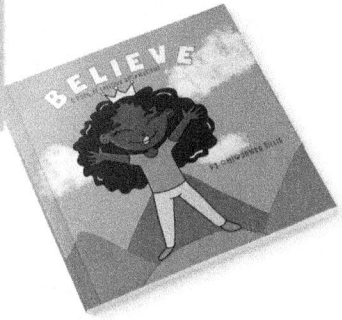
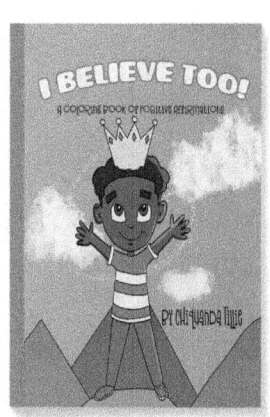
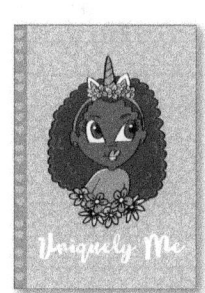
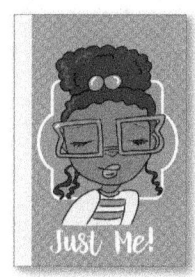
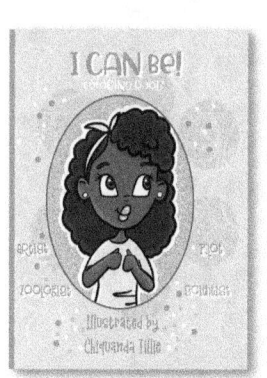
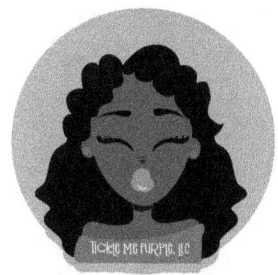

## Color With Me

*Tickle Me Purple, LLC*

www.ticklemepurple.com